FV

PERSPECTIVES

A Multicultural Portrait of
Life in the Cities

By David K. Wright

Marshall Cavendish
New York • London • Toronto

Cover: The busy streets and colorful sights of Chinatown, San Francisco.

Published by
Marshall Cavendish Corporation
2415 Jerusalem Avenue
P.O. Box 587
North Bellmore, New York 11710, USA

© Marshall Cavendish Corporation, 1994

Edited, designed, and produced by Water Buffalo Books, Milwaukee

Project director: Mark Sachner
Art director: Sabine Beaupré
Picture researcher: Diane Laska
Indexer: Valerie Weber
Marshall Cavendish development editor: MaryLee Knowlton
Marshall Cavendish editorial director: Evelyn Fazio

Editorial consultants: Mark S. Guardalabene, Milwaukee Public Schools; Yolanda Ayubi, Ph.D., Consultant on Ethnic Issues, U.S. Department of Labor

Picture Credits: © Archive Photos: 9, 11 (middle and bottom), 19 (top), 32 (both), 35 (top), 41, 42 (top), 45 (top), 48 (bottom), 63 (bottom), 70 (both); © Archive Photos/American Stock: 18 (bottom), 25 (top), 43; © Archive Photos/Frank Driggs Collections: 45 (bottom); © Archive Photos/Michael V. Guthrie: 28 (both); © Archive Photos/Imapress: 59 (top); © Archive Photos/Levick: 14; © Archive Photos/Florence Parker: 37 (top); © Archive Photos/Edward Rice: 19 (bottom); © Archive Photos/P. L. Sperr: 57; © Archive Photos/VALS: 18 (top); © Bill Bachmann/Third Coast Stock Source: 67 (middle and bottom); © Darryl Baird/Third Coast Stock Source: 51 (bottom); Sabine Beaupré, 1993: 17 (top); © Nancy Hoyt Belcher/Photo Network: 29 (top); © Marion Bernstein/Picture Perfect USA: 75 (bottom); © The Bettmann Archive: 8, 10 (both), 12, 16, 17 (bottom), 24, 40 (top), 72; © Win Brookhouse/Photo Network: 58; © Charles Phelps Cushing/H. Armstrong Roberts: 64; © Culver Pictures: 40 (bottom); © Grace Davies/Photo Network: 6; © Jeff Dunn/Picture Perfect USA: 75 (top); © Bob Firth/International Stock: Cover, 49 (top); © T. J. Florian/Photo Network: 21 (bottom), 29 (middle); Courtesy of the Florida Department of Commerce, Division of Tourism: 62 (both); © William B. Folsom/Picture Perfect USA: 68; © Ewing Galloway: 30; © Dennis Giampaolo/Photo Network: 22; © Frank Grant/International Stock: 49 (bottom); © Tom and Michele Grimm/International Stock: 29 (bottom); © Michael J. Howell/International Stock: 51 (top); © Dave and Les Jacobs/Picture Perfect USA: 46, 60; © R. Kord/H. Armstrong Roberts: 71 (top); © Michael E. Lubiarz/Picture Perfect USA: 38; © Michael Philip Manheim/Photo Network: 11 (top); © Tom McCarthy Photos/Photo Network: 66; © Ken Osburn/Third Coast Stock Source: 54; © Photo Network: 25 (middle and bottom); © Barry Pribula/International Stock: 67 (top); © Alon Reininger/Photo Network: 73; © Jack Riesland/Picture Perfect USA: 50; © H. Armstrong Roberts: 13, 21 (top), 26 (top), 33, 42 (bottom), 48 (top), 71 (bottom); © John Sanford/Photo Network: 53; © Lindsay Silverman/International Stock: 63 (top); © Craig Skorburg: 37 (bottom); © Joe Sohm-Chromosohm/Picture Perfect USA: 59 (bottom); © Universal City Studios/Photo Network: 26 (bottom); Jim Wend/collection of Moshe ben-Shimon: 44, 52; © Bobbe Wolf/International Stock: 35 (bottom)

Library of Congress Cataloging-in-Publication Data

Wright, David K.
    A multicultural portrait of life in the cities / David K. Wright.
        p.   cm. — (Perspectives)
    Includes bibliographical references and index.
    Summary: Discusses the history of such cities as New York, San Francisco, Detroit, and Miami, particularly from the vantage point of women and minorities.
    ISBN 1-85435-659-3 :
    1. Minorities—United States—History—Juvenile literature. 2. Cities and towns—United States—History—Juvenile literature. 3. City and town life—United States—History—Juvenile literature. 4. United States—Race relations—Juvenile literature. 5. United States—Ethnic relations—Juvenile literature. [1. Cities and towns—History. 2. Minorities—History. 3. Ethnic relations.]
I. Title. II. Series: Perspectives (Marshall Cavendish Corporation)
E184.A1W84   1993
305.8'00973—dc20   93-10318
                                                                                        CIP
                                                                                        AC

To PS – MS

Printed and bound in the U.S.A.

CONTENTS

About *Perspectives*

Perspectives is a series of multicultural portraits of events and topics in U.S. history. Each volume examines these events and topics not only from the perspective of the white European-Americans who make up the majority of the U.S. population, but also from that of the nation's many people of color and other ethnic minorities, such as African-Americans, Asian-Americans, Hispanic-Americans, and American Indians. These people, along with women, have been given little attention in traditional accounts of U.S. history. And yet their impact on historical events has been great.

The terms *American Indian*, *Hispanic-American*, *Anglo-American*, *African-American*, *Black*, and *Asian-American*, like *European-American* and *white*, are used by the authors in this series to identify people of various national origins. Labeling people is a serious business, and what we call a group depends on many things. For example, a few decades ago it was considered acceptable to use the words *colored* or *Negro* to label people of African origin. Today, these words are outdated and often a sign of ignorance or outright prejudice. Some people even consider *Black* less acceptable than *African-American* because it focuses on a person's skin color rather than national origins. And yet *Black* has many practical uses, particularly to describe people whose origins are not only African but Caribbean or Latin American as well.

If we must label people, it's better to be as specific as possible. That is a goal of *Perspectives* — to be as precise and fair as possible in the labeling of people by race, ethnicity, national origin, or other factors, such as gender or disability. When necessary and possible, Americans of Mexican origin will be called *Mexican-Americans*. Americans of Irish origin will be called *Irish-Americans*, and so on. The same goes for American Indians: when possible, specific Indians are identified by their tribal names, such as the *Chippewa* or *Mohawk*. But in a discussion of various Indian groups, tribal origins may not always be entirely clear, and so it may be more practical to use *American Indian*, a term that has widespread use among Indians and non-Indians alike.

Even within a group, individuals may disagree over the names they prefer for their group: *Black* or *African-American*? *American Indian* or *native American*? *Hispanic* or *Latino*? *White*, *Anglo*, or *European-American*? Different situations often call for different labels. The labels used in *Perspectives* represent an attempt to be fair, accurate, and perhaps most importantly, to be mindful of what people choose to call *themselves*.

A Note About *Life in the Cities*

Reading about the following cities will give readers a chance to check their own perceptions of where American cities came from, what they have come to be, and where they are headed.

New York City. New York's eighteen million area residents are steeped in many histories — of immigration, culture, communications, and the arts. For all its size, however, it is fragile, with tenuous ethnic relations and millions of people putting a strain on the city's deteriorating services and contributing to landfills as far away as the Midwest.

Los Angeles. Second in size only to New York City, Los Angeles is seen by scholars as a preview of cities in the next century, with its mix of cultures, rancid air, and thousands of small, ingenious, cottage-industry jobs.

Chicago. This "capital" of the Midwest is a city of European-Americans and African-Americans in a state filled with people of Appalachian and colonial American descent. Chicago's strengths are in its diversified industry, transportation, and dozens of ethnic neighborhoods, which can sometimes be pockets of ethnic isolation and intolerance.

Detroit. Both praised and insulted as America's first Third World city, Detroit has huge problems. Yet it offers opportunity, too, particularly for African-Americans to run a city as they choose. Can this metropolis beset by financial and social woes rise again, this time without the economic help of the now-troubled automobile industry?

San Francisco. Surrounded by water and suburbs, the only direction San Francisco can grow is up. Despite being near a major earthquake fault line, San Francisco's frequent fogs, air-conditioned climate, tolerance of people of various cultures and orientations, and spotless neighborhoods continue to lure visitors.

New Orleans. New Orleans, while as exotic as San Francisco, is less prosperous and a bit more dangerous, at least after the sun goes down. It is also an exciting mix of cultures, a steamy place where people care about preserving the past, what's on the menu, and having a musical good time. In some ways New Orleans is the most American of cities, in other ways the least.

Miami. Shimmering in the sun, Miami is full of possibilities, not all of them safe or legal. In fact, because it is a transportation center Miami also is an intersection for drug-smuggling, gun-running, and other illicit activities. Big buildings prod the skyline as people from Europe, the Caribbean, and Central and South America spend more and more time there.

San Antonio. How could such a nice city arise from the arid landscape of south-central Texas? America's largest city with a Hispanic-American majority is also the country's ninth-largest metropolitan area. It has an inviting downtown riverwalk and an average year-round temperature of sixty-eight degrees.

As a group, these cities make up a composite portrait of the ethnic, geographical, historical, and cultural diversity found in virtually all U.S. cities.

Mayan ruins in Mexico, remnants of a great civilization.

CHAPTER ONE

Centers of Humanity

The soldiers under Francisco Vasquez de Coronado were unimpressed with the first pueblo they came across in 1540 as they searched for seven fabled cities of gold. The drab little population center under a cliff in what is now New Mexico held none of the riches a Spanish priest claimed to have seen with his own eyes. The *conquistadores* (conquerors) cursed the priest.

In contrast, the first Spaniards to set eyes on the Mayan or Aztec or Incan civilizations were stunned. Magnificent pyramids pointed skyward. Temples and monasteries towered above the populace. Palaces had been specially constructed for the ruling class. There were even large, paved areas set aside for games that resembled basketball and baths in which to relax after a hard-fought athletic event.

Mayan Accomplishments

At the time of Christ, the Mayan civilization in what is now southeastern Mexico was at least as advanced as the civilizations of Egypt, the Middle East, Europe, or India. The native people, whose descendants would one day be called *Indians* by their Spanish conquerors, conceived the mathematical idea of zero. They constructed stone buildings, using precise formulas to ensure that the curves and angles matched. They created a calendar that was exact to within one day every 374,000 years. And they crafted costumes, jewelry, and other art that compare with anything made today. The inhabitants of southern North America also had a written language. Modern-era scientists would puzzle over these hieroglyphs for years before understanding the pictorial language.

The Mayan downfall — and the downfall of the Aztecs and other advanced Central and South American native civilizations — was the inability to fend off Spaniards armed with guns or to survive diseases brought to the Western Hemisphere by the Europeans. Why were these native cultures so advanced when the Indians who lived in what is now North America built no gleaming palaces and carved no brilliant jewelry? Part of the answer lies in the scientific ability of the Mayans, and part of the answer lies in geography.

Science Leads to Growth

These Mayan Indians looked at the skies, decided there were patterns to the motions of the Sun, Moon, stars, and planets, and, after years of study, believed there were preferred times to plant, cultivate, and harvest crops. Their predictions proved to be correct, resulting in crop surpluses. The surplus crops in turn gave the Mayans time to construct buildings, design jewelry, perform elaborate religious ceremonies, and more. Indians farther north tended to be nomadic hunters who followed huge herds of buffalo, elk, and other animals. Attempting to live permanently in a city would have driven away these sources of food, clothing, and trade. Frequent moves made for few possessions, none of them permanent.

There were other reasons why such native American groups as the Inuit in the north, the Sioux in the Plains, and the Iroquois in the forests erected no cities worthy of the name. They had no materials that compared to the stone used by Central and South American Indians. The Inuit constructed homes from materials that were available — chunks of ice, driftwood, and bone. The Sioux and other Plains people made almost everything they owned out of the meat and hides and bones of the wild animals they killed for food. And while forest Indians raised corn, beans, pumpkins, and other vegetables, crops weren't large because the growing season was short.

Yet amid the lush center of North America there arose some two thousand years ago a city truly worthy of the name. The site was conceived by the Moundbuilders, a people that made enormous sculptured mounds out of earth. These shapes of birds or serpents were up to 3.5 miles long and covered as much as one hundred acres.

Near what is now St. Louis, Missouri, the Moundbuilders in about A.D. 500 created a city that held an estimated thirty thousand residents. It had a pyramid with a broader base than the Great Pyramid of Egypt, and the city, called Cahokia, featured toolmakers, hide processors, potters, jewelrymakers, weavers, and engravers. Other tribes elsewhere mastered irrigation, weaving cotton from cloth, and ceramics.

Plains Indians hunted buffalo and other wildlife.

Comparing American Indian cities to cities in Europe, Africa, and elsewhere is akin to comparing apples and oranges. Such African places as Benin, Cairo, Kilwa, and Timbuktu were highly advanced, complete with ironmakers, weavers, ceramicists, sculptors, and skilled farmers. European cities grew first in response to trade, while centers of Mayan civilization were intended primarily for religious observation and for the pleasure of the ruling class. Most Mayans lived around their cities in simple huts. Yet they came together in cities at regular intervals, primarily to watch and to react as religious sacrifices were made.

Colonial America's First City

Early European-American settlements weren't much to see. St. Augustine, Florida, the first European settlement in what would become the U.S., was founded by Ponce de Leon in 1513. But there were no buildings on the site until the French erected a fort, without sanitary facilities or much else but four walls, in 1564. Spain reclaimed the area in 1565, and St. Augustine would be the northernmost point of Spain's colonial empire for the next 256 years. But it was only a crude stone jail, with soldiers and prisoners dependent on the nearby St. John's River for drinking water and everything else. When the site finally fell into U.S. hands in 1821, it became a grimy jail for hostile Indians.

The first permanent English-speaking settlement in North America was Jamestown, founded in 1607 by Captain James Smith and 105 soldiers in what today is Virginia. By 1619, English settlers had formed a legislature called the House of Burgesses (representatives). The following year, 103 Pilgrims who wished to separate from the Church of England intended to settle in Virginia but instead landed at Plymouth, in what is today Massachusetts. The Pilgrims immediately drew up a document called the *Mayflower Compact*, named for the ship that brought them to America. The agreement stated that the immigrants would form a government and abide by its laws. Like the government taking shape in Jamestown, the Pilgrims' pact was intended only for free adult males. Sadly, half of all new residents died during the first harsh Massachusetts winter.

Death visited the Indians even more frequently than the European settlers. Since Indians weren't Christians, otherwise pious whites, such as the Puritans who came to Massachusetts after the Pilgrims, felt no guilt when it came to killing them in huge numbers. Nor did they feel it wrong to lie to the Indians to get them to lay down their arms prior to a massacre. In one especially gory Massachusetts day, six hundred Pequot men, women, and children were burned to death or cut to pieces with swords and pikes. This was only one of several attacks on the Pequots, whose major sin was being in the way of European

The Prophet

No one could stop the flood of immigrants who came to America in the 1800s. But The Prophet, his brother Tecumseh, and other determined American Indians slowed the move west and the encroachment of Europeans onto native lands.

The Prophet, whose real name was Tenskwatawa, was born in what is now Ohio in 1768. A Shawnee, he and Tecumseh tried to halt encroachment in the Northwest Territories — what we know today as the Midwest.

The Indian leader denounced individual ownership, alcohol consumption, wearing textiles rather than skins and furs, and Indian-European marriages.

The Prophet's message was strong. But it was not strong enough. Tecumseh was the superior military man, yet The Prophet let his people be drawn into battle in 1811 while Tecumseh was away. The confederacy of tribes destroyed, his followers ceased to hold The Prophet in awe. He died in 1834 in Kansas, where he had moved as white settlers continued their push west.

expansion. After the massacre, the Puritans gave thanks to God for their speedy victory. Sadly, this kind of conduct was repeated by well-armed English, French, and Spanish men.

Those who believe American cities grew because of slave labor have a strong argument. In 1800, for example, there were only 5.3 million persons of European descent in the United States. In contrast, there were at least 10 million slaves and possibly as many as 15 million. Large plantations often had half a dozen or fewer whites and perhaps fifty African slaves of all ages and of both sexes. Had slave importation not been outlawed in 1808, the country could easily have an African-American majority today. Despite the ban, an estimated 250,000 slaves were smuggled into the country between 1808 and 1860. It's no exaggeration to say that southern agriculture could not have worked without slavery and that even northern cities depended on slaves and free Blacks for some of their growth. It's also not surprising that among wealthy British and American colonists, a real worry was the threat of conspiracy between slaves and poor whites.

Centers of Humanity

Since time began, cities have shared many of the same assets and liabilities. Enemies have no trouble finding cities in time of war, but no city ever completely surrenders to an invading army. Disease spreads quickly where there are groups of people, but so do ideas. Cities are centers of commerce and trade, and people willing to risk living in a city (with its constant stench of sewage) learned whether their skills could be marketed. A wonderful cook could trade food for pottery. A sharp-eyed wanderer in the woods could swap her collection of moss and mushrooms for a freshly tanned hide. Cities are usually on bodies of water, and as such are points of entry that people must pass through. Travelers to and from cities could trade their experiences for food and a place to sleep. Cities became magnets for all that is best and worst about humankind. This was true of the cities in colonial America, and it would certainly prove to be true of the cities that would sprout all across the fledgling U.S. and help mold the personality of a new nation.

America as Utopia —
The New Migrations

Top: A Puritan couple hides from nearby Indians.
Bottom: An African slave in a cotton field.

If you were white and European, you were free to dream up the most eccentric idea for a city and then try to interest others in the scheme. In populated areas, believers in new religions such as Mormonism were bedeviled by suspicious neighbors. Even mainstream religions could be dangerous: nineteen persons were put to death in Salem, Massachusetts, in 1692 by preachers attacking witchcraft.

Brigham Young knew of the potential for harm to a religious minority long before he set eyes on the Great Salt Lake in what is today Utah. A rivalry had developed among the leaders of the Mormon church following the killing of founder Joseph Smith, murdered by Illinois militiamen in 1844. After Smith's death, most Mormons decided to follow Young west in his search for a safe and sacred place to settle. But now Young was under pressure. The believers had been chased out of settlements in Missouri and Illinois, and Young probably knew the followers would not hold still for many more lengthy moves.

In the winter of 1846-47, the column of Mormons wound slowly westward until the leaders stopped at a site overlooking a vast, arid valley that included a huge lake. "This is the place," Young told other church leaders. The Mormons descended into the valley where, despite hardships, they went to work building their church and their city. So long as they were in the majority, who would oppose them?

Scenes like this, which featured people committed either to new religions or to new social systems, were repeated over and over in the United States as the population grew. Schemes harbored in places such as England or Scotland or Switzerland blossomed into socialist or religious communities such as New Harmony, Indiana, or New Lebanon, New York, or Lancaster, Pennsylvania. But not all religious and social movements came from abroad; several were entirely American inspirations.

Besides Joseph Smith, the founder of Mormonism, whose teachings came to him in the form of biblical-like revelations on stone slabs and visits from an angel, religious communities were led by such persons as Mary Baker Eddy, Anna Lee, and William Miller. Eddy began Christian Science, a religion that promoted healing by spiritual methods. Anna Lee started the Shakers, who died out as a group, in part because they gave up sex and therefore failed to produce new members. William Miller began the Seventh-day Adventists, a denomination whose principles include the belief that the end of the world and the return of Christ to be close at hand. The most successful new beliefs were versions of Christianity.

Utopia's Legacy

Though utopian communities usually failed, they left behind ideas that are still current. Robert Owen, a British manufacturer, purchased Harmonie,

Top: The Mormon Temple in modern Salt Lake City, Utah. *Middle:* Brigham Young. *Bottom:* Joseph Smith.

William Penn negotiates a treaty with American Indians.

Indiana, from another group of utopians known as Rappites. He established a cooperative community, believing that his was superior to the communal living practiced in most other planned communities. Though Owen's scheme failed, his followers opened the first U.S. kindergarten, the first trade school, the first free library, and the first community-supported school. Clearly, the public could learn and benefit from some utopian practices.

A careful reading of the U.S. Constitution shows the document to be an invitation to religious cults and social experiments. The Bill of Rights (the first ten constitutional amendments) promises freedom of religion, speech, and the press; a measure of privacy; and control in areas not delegated to the federal government. Europeans, particularly religious dissenters, paid close attention to the wording. Equally important, young followers learned that land was inexpensive and that there was plenty of it. Utopian communities wanted to end greed; it was easy to share and be generous in this land of plenty.

Unfortunately, not everyone in young America was equal. Indians were cheated or killed. Slaves were not counted as human beings, and only white adult males were allowed to vote for their political representatives. Women, children, and people with disabilities were ignored. Some utopians, however, treated minorities with respect. William Penn, a Quaker, signed a treaty in 1683 with the Delaware Indians and paid them for land he wanted to occupy. Oberlin College, a Quaker institution in Ohio, was a pioneer in admitting African-American students, enrolling them before the Civil War.

Other Dreams

Others came to America and helped build the cities for different reasons. Revolutionary activity swept much of Europe in 1848, and persons who led such disruptions were sought by the police. It only made sense to flee Europe, with its monarchies, its lack of space, and its rigid social systems, for a roomier, more democratic place. Some immigrants, particularly the Irish, suffered not only repression but disease or famine, and left their homes as a result. Popular destinations included Australia, Canada, and, of course, the United States. Sons and daughters of radicals and revolutionaries would organize labor, look after new immigrants, and raise up huge metropolises where there had been forests a few years before.

Not all immigrants came across the Atlantic Ocean. For centuries, the overpopulation of China had put pressure on that country. Chinese began to

What was the world's first city?

The answer to this question could change as archeologists continue to excavate ancient civilizations. At the moment the very first settlement that could be called a city is Jericho, in what is today the Israeli-occupied West Bank. Six miles north of the Dead Sea and more than eight hundred feet below sea level, Jericho is in an area that is unbearably hot in the late spring, summer, and early fall and can be uncomfortably chilly in the winter. It hardly seems an ideal site for a town.

Yet a town it was, as early as 9000 B.C. Perhaps Jericho grew because of a large spring there with fresh water, a rarity in the Jordan Valley. It isn't a large stretch of imagination to envision wanderers coming across this source of life and deciding to stay through hot and cold weather in an otherwise very dry land. After a brief period of living in flimsy huts, the inhabitants built solid houses of mud, then other buildings of stone.

A massive stone wall was constructed around the ten-acre site in about 8000 B.C. There is evidence that the residents irrigated crops outside the walls with their precious source of water. Pieces of art have been recovered in the area, and there is also evidence that architecture became more elaborate. People from as far away as northern Syria came to live in Jericho, and other nomads wandered in and stayed or kept going as the years passed.

The town came under Roman influence, and several large and elaborate buildings went up — often on top of older buildings. The wall around the city was rebuilt several times, and it is this wall that the biblical Joshua and his Israelite followers knocked down in battle. The town faded into obscurity for much of the last two thousand years, but it did house hundreds of Arab refugees following the creation of the state of Israel in 1949. Much of the town's population left after the 1967 Arab-Israeli War, and there are only about seven thousand persons in Jericho today.

leave their homeland in earnest as early as the fifteenth century, and the first Chinese immigrants to the United States landed in California in the 1840s. They held no illusions about a utopia, and they performed jobs no one else wanted — as miners, launderers, seamstresses, and laborers.

Construction of the first transcontinental railroad in 1869 was finished, at least in the West, by ten thousand Chinese and three thousand Irish immigrants. Most other residents of northern California preferred to look for gold and continued their search long after the strike of 1848. Since individual prospectors really could strike it rich, why lay rails across hot and hostile territory for one to two dollars a day?

In the wake of such restrictive laws as the Chinese Exclusion Act of 1882, Congress sharply curbed immigration in 1921, setting up a quota system that favored white Europeans — especially western Europeans — and discriminated against everyone else. U.S. immigration law was updated in 1990 and is now based on numbers of persons being issued visas rather than on where someone is from. Half a million persons a year, plus refugees, now are given residence in the U.S. Preferences are given to relatives of U.S. citizens and to those with job skills needed in this country. Most of the newest Americans will live at least for a time in U.S. cities. Some will live in the cities examined in detail in the chapters that follow.

Joyful immigrants get their first glimpse of Ellis Island and the Statue of Liberty in the New York City harbor.

New York City

The middle-aged Jewish couple peered down the line of immigrants toward the tall, uniformed Americans. The uniformed men peered down throats and into eyes and ears, checking for — what? Tuberculosis, jaundice, hereditary disease? Most immigrants passed inspection and went joyously out the door onto Ellis Island in New York Bay. But a few were sent sorrowfully for closer examination into offices at the side of the big, echoing building.

The pair from Poland were confident of their health because the husband was a doctor. He had kept himself, his wife, and their neighborhood in the city of Lublin healthy for twenty-five years. Now, because their children were grown, and because the couple could no longer tolerate the constant anti-Semitism, they had decided to emigrate. Better a happy peddler than an unhappy physician, the doctor thought on that warm day in 1896.

One of the men in uniform grabbed the couple's papers and flipped through them as the other looked the two over for signs of disease. "Shmuel? That's not much of a name. I can't even read the last name," he said aloud, beginning to write. "Everything's filled out, looks good. There — now you're Sam Lublin. And Sarah. That sounds better, more American. Go on." He handed back the papers. In a split second, without understanding a word of English, the immigrant couple had become different people as they walked quickly outside to see who awaited them.

Immigration at Its Peak

Hundreds of thousands of Jews and others came to America under similar circumstances in the late nineteenth and early twentieth centuries. At its peak, Ellis Island processed eight thousand European immigrants a week. Most settled, at least initially, in and around New York City. These first-generation Americans saw something in New York that had been evident to Europeans since 1624, when the Dutch bought the island of Manhattan from American Indians for sixty guilders (about 2,400 English cents) worth of tools and trinkets. The Dutch called the area New Amsterdam and soon began to parcel out immense estates to their favorites up and down the beautiful Hudson River, and the English did the same after taking control in 1661.

Immigrant families often were large and poor.

The first Jewish settlers had arrived a few years earlier. They came from an intolerant, Catholic Spain by way of a more tolerant, Protestant Netherlands. Jews, in fact, can trace their roots in America back further than most: five of Columbus's crew are said to have been Spanish Jews, though they had been forced to convert to Christianity. A small number of Jews from Brazil arrived in New Amsterdam in 1654. They had left Europe for Brazil when the vast South American colony was under Portuguese rule but decided to move after the Dutch seized control from the Portuguese.

In 1643, less than twenty years after the sale of Manhattan to the Dutch, a Catholic missionary reported hearing eighteen different languages during a stroll through the city! As it grew, New York became a raucous city of extremes, with a few immensely rich persons of English descent owning thousands of acres on one hand and people from all over the world with nothing on the other. As the largest city in colonial America, New York also had the biggest debtor's prison. Many colonists who sided with the British during the Revolution did so because the British practiced a hands-off policy when it came to dealing with the wealthy, preferring to tax the less influential.

In addition to its sizable population of poor Europeans, the city had the largest northern slave population both before and after the American Revolution. A slave revolt in 1712 resulted in six suicides and twenty-one executions. New York's African-Americans rose up again in 1741 over the way in which they were worked, housed, and fed. A total of twenty-six slaves lost their lives and seventy-one were deported after the 1741 uprising.

When the British left New York in 1783, they took with them three thousand slaves who had served British troops during the war. Even with this large exodus, there remained many slaves in New York. After the Revolution, the free Black population of New York City lagged behind that of Boston or Philadelphia because free Blacks did not want to live in a city where they might be mistaken for slaves and servants. As a result, there were thriving African-American neighborhoods in many other northern cities well before such neighborhoods existed in New York.

Five Boroughs Make a City

The city continued to grow during the 1800s, taking the shape we know today. New York City is made up of five boroughs, which operate as counties as well as making up a single city. They are Manhattan (New York County), the Bronx, Brooklyn (Kings County), Queens, and Staten Island (Richmond

County). Manhattan is one of the world's best-known islands. Brooklyn and Queens are on the western end of Long Island, and Staten Island hugs the shore of nearby New Jersey. Only the Bronx, immediately north of Manhattan, is not on an island.

A Turbulent Town

New Yorkers have always been quick to complain if they feel they've been wronged. An extreme example is the rioting that took place during the Civil War in 1863. Whites protested the fact that well-to-do persons could avoid military service by paying a sum of money. The rioters also turned their wrath on innocent Blacks, hanging several by the time they were through rampaging. Before such payment arrangements ended in 1864, about a thousand rioters had been killed by the police and militia.

In the 1870s one politician, William Marcy "Boss" Tweed, and his hand-picked cronies stole an estimated $30–$200 million from the city. Tweed died in jail, but this was money that could have been used elsewhere. That became evident in a book, *How the Other Half Lives*, that appeared in 1890. Written by Jacob Riis, an immigrant himself and a police reporter for a New York newspaper, this muckraking work exposed just how miserable were the lives of many immigrants. Riis used a recent invention, a camera with flashbulbs, to back his words, which stated that some tenements on the Lower East Side had an infant death rate of 10 percent. The Danish native's book caused the state to legislate against the worst slum conditions.

Ellis Island opened as an immigration depot two years later. Persons who passed through on the way to New York City could count on gradually improved housing, but working conditions often were terrible. Unions such as the International Ladies' Garment Workers Union formed in New York City in 1900, yet there continued to be terrible mishaps in the workplace. Among the worst was the Triangle shirt factory fire in the city in 1911. Some 145 young, immigrant seamstresses, working long hours for low wages, were trapped and killed when fire swept the seedy, tenth-story factory. The tragedy led to more legislation and better working conditions.

When people recall turbulent times, they most often are thinking about things that went on in big cities. The year 1920 was such a time, with 2,700 anarchists, communists, and other radicals arrested nationwide, many of them in New York City. A bit later, in September, a bomb exploded in Wall Street, killing thirty persons, injuring one hundred, and serving as a comment by radicals on the American economic and political system. Despite gains on certain fronts, such as the fact that women were given the right to vote

New York City is made up of five boroughs — the Bronx, Brooklyn, Manhattan, Queens, and Staten Island.

Photo of a nineteenth-century New York City tenement sweat shop, from the Jacob Riis book *How the Other Half Lives.*

A skylight in the circular Guggenheim Museum.

and the League of Women Voters was formed that same year, in many ways the system at the time was not working well: the U.S. and most other countries were in a short but deep recession following World War I.

The Culture Capital

New York was not all squalor and despair, even in times of economic hardship. The city in 1913 was dazzled by the New York Armory Show, which for the first time brought modern, abstract art to the United States from Europe. Thereafter, the city grew to become a world leader in art tastes and movements. Within walking distance of each other today are the Museum of Modern Art on West Fifty-third Street, the Metropolitan Museum of Art at Fifth Avenue and Eighty-second Street, and the Guggenheim Museum at Fifth Avenue and Eighty-ninth Street. The city has hundreds of large and small galleries, and the residents know and enjoy the history of Western art.

New York lost ground to California in the 1920s as the moviemaking capital, though the first sound-on-film motion picture, *Phonofilm*, was introduced at the Rivoli Theater in New York City in 1923. Radio had millions of listeners by the end of the decade, and composers such as George Gershwin wrote stunning pieces for symphony orchestra play and broadcast. Gershwin's *Rhapsody in Blue* was first heard in 1924. By 1927, the musical *Show Boat* was vying for audiences with movies such as *The Jazz Singer*, which starred Al Jolson. The city established itself as the country's magazine and book-publishing center as New York firms brought forth in the 1920s and 1930s work by such notable writers as Thomas Wolfe, Gertrude Stein, William Faulkner, Ernest Hemingway, Willa Cather, and F. Scott Fitzgerald.

Few people had any money in the 1930s, and New York City became a magic place in the mind of the average American, who saw smartly dressed, smart-talking, wealthy, handsome people portrayed as New Yorkers in the movies. Big bands blared out tunes named after actual New York telephone numbers ("Pennsylvania 6-5000") and such destinations as Times Square, Grand Central Station, and under the clock at the Biltmore Hotel were nationally known locales. Other cities may have held ticker-tape parades following World War II, but the gala thrown by New York overshadowed them all.

In fact, everything about New York has always seemed larger than life, including the tragedies. On July 28, 1945, a U.S. Army Air Corps B-25 bomber flew into the side of the Empire State Building, the tallest structure in the world at the time. The plane could be seen, from hundreds of feet below in the street, sticking out of the side of the skyscraper! In 1980 former Beatle John Lennon was shot to death on the street outside his New York

Al Jolson as *The Jazz Singer.*

City apartment. And in 1990 an after-hours social club in a Latino section of the city was firebombed, leaving eighty-seven persons dead.

A City with a Jewish Influence

About 40 percent of all New Yorkers say they are Roman Catholics, while only 10 percent call themselves Jews. Yet from pushcarts to politics and from bagels to show biz and the arts, Jews have shaped the city as has no other ethnic or religious group. Contrary to many stereotypes and despite their common religious roots, New York's Jewish population cuts across a variety of class lines. An ethnic as much as a religious group, New York Jews also represent a fascinating mix of the cultures and movements that shape Judaism itself.

During the time when most Jews in New York came from various parts of Europe, most practicing Jews were Orthodox. And even in today's New York, where Jewishness is not merely tolerated but experienced far more openly than in any other Western city, Orthodox Jews have kept alive Jewish learning as it has been studied and lived for centuries.

Perhaps no Orthodox Jewish group has pursued its concept of Jewish life — and its belief in the coming of the messiah — with as much passion and piety as have Hasidic Jews. With their distinctive — and for males, predominantly black — attire, Hasidim are by far the most easily recognized of all Jews. More importantly, their way of dressing, like their way of life, is an example of the Hasidic concentration on religion and the laws they believe God established for humankind.

In New York, as in many larger cities in North America, Hasidim take jobs that will keep them in or near the home, the better to build a close-knit community. In some neighborhoods, such as the Crown Heights area of Brooklyn, Hasidim patrol their own streets and enforce their own codes of behavior. This furthers their sense of community, but it has also put a strain on their relations with other minorities, particularly Blacks, who share the close quarters of New York's crowded neighborhoods.

In an age when Jews have become increasingly blended into American society, many have turned to Reform or Conservative Judaism, which are Judaism's two largest branches. Less strictly observant of Jewish law, many Jews have chosen on their own to participate in the rituals and traditions of Jewish life. Most of these Jews, like Jews throughout the United States, are the children and grandchildren of New York's Ellis Island.

Life in Harlem

African-Americans have also had an extraordinary influence, both in body and in spirit, on the life of New York City. Harlem is the largest single concentration of Black people in America. It was the site in the 1920s of a wonderful cultural period called the Harlem Renaissance that changed African-American literature and art from an imitation of work produced by European-Americans to original work that emphasized racial pride and confidence. Though the Great Depression of the 1930s forced many writers and artists to scatter, their influence continues to be felt in this huge community.

Below: Spanish East Harlem.
Bottom: Young residents of Harlem.

A rose in Harlem

Homelessness, AIDS, drug addiction — not subjects that usually lead to stories with happy endings — especially stories of people for whom these conditions go hand in hand. But hope and compassion have bloomed in an unlikely setting.

Standup Harlem sprang up amidst the poverty and hopelessness of a Harlem neighborhood where crack and heroin are abundant, but housing and care for homeless people with AIDS have been scarce. With the right treatment and care, many people whose immune systems are weakened by AIDS or HIV (the virus that causes AIDS) can fight off infections and illnesses for years. But homeless people who are infected with HIV often get sick and die more quickly from AIDS because they cannot get the same care.

Housed in an eleven-room brownstone, Standup Harlem welcomes anyone who needs a place to eat and live. And if that person is infected with HIV or addicted to drugs, then the welcome is so much the greater. At Standup Harlem, people come in off of the streets for nourishment that is both physical and emotional. Many attend meetings of Narcotics Anonymous and other support groups, and they get good food and free medical care.

Just as inspiring as the stories that have come *out* of Standup Harlem is the story of what went *into* Standup Harlem. In 1989 Louis Jones, a homeless, thirty-six-year-old heroin addict, made a big decision. It was time not only to stop using drugs, but to figure out what to do with his life now that he had tested positive for HIV. Paula Palmateer's credentials were quite different. A forty-seven-year-old business executive from Colorado, she had never even visited New York until 1989. But unable to turn her back on what would become almost a sacred mission, she returned to do volunteer work at homeless shelters. There, she met Mr. Jones. At first, they had trouble getting landlords to go along with their plans. But with courage, vision, and help from various grants and loans, they bought a rundown building and accomplished an inspirational goal — restoring a house to a noble purpose in life and restoring hope to human lives.

Equally significant was an earlier movement — the founding of the National Association for the Advancement of Colored People, or NAACP. In 1908, New York City Blacks believed the treatment of their race had reached its low point. A mob of whites had killed dozens of African-Americans in Springfield, Illinois, the former home of Abraham Lincoln. Elsewhere, there were written and unwritten laws denying African-Americans equal treatment. Some sixty Black and white persons gathered in New York and formed a civil rights organization that played a huge role in the movement to overcome racial segregation in the 1950s and 1960s. Today, the NAACP has more than 500,000 members.

Despite the accomplishments of groups like the NAACP, racism and poverty have put down roots in inner-city America that have outlasted many positive effects of the civil rights movement. Today, many argue that drugs and guns and crime have done more harm to Harlem than any organization has done good. Though the huge area on the northwestern edge of Manhattan is crumbling, there continue to be smaller neighborhoods within the community that have succeeded in keeping their streets safer and their buildings secure. Yet the streets can be dangerous day or night for persons of any age or background. Despite the efforts of many community groups, the effects of cocaine may be tougher to overcome than centuries of prejudice.

North America's oldest and most exciting mainland Puerto Rican community is next door in East (or Spanish) Harlem. Just north of New York City's wealthy Upper East Side, the area is two hundred blocks in size and has about 120,000 residents. Spanish Harlem has a culture of its own — a rich and vibrant hybrid of New York street life and Puerto Rican influences in art, music, food, and fashion. Unfortunately, high crime and school-dropout rates are also common, with the deadly potential of gunfire or drugs on many corners. As in many urban neighborhoods, the threat of AIDS has spawned a campaign to teach people about HIV/AIDS and to help people who may be at high risk or who already have HIV.

Bounded by Fifth Avenue on the west and the Harlem River on the east, East Harlem formerly was home to first-generation Jews and Italians. Today, speculators are buying up portions of East Harlem, forcing poorer residents to look for vacancies in public housing where and if available. In addition to East Harlem, the 860,000 Puerto Ricans in all of New York reside primarily in Brooklyn and the Bronx.

Still a Rich Mix

It is possible to find almost any ethnic group at all in New York City — if you're willing to look. A group of Mohawk Indians migrated to Brooklyn in the 1920s to sign on as ironworkers, building huge bridges, the Empire State Building, and other skyscrapers. Their superior sense of balance and agility was first noticed on a bridge constructed across the St. Lawrence River between Canada and the United States. The Mohawks later came south to join construction crews working hundreds of feet above Manhattan's streets and rivers. Though many have left their Brooklyn neighborhood, they have also left their mark on the city's skyline.

According to one recent survey, today's New York City is about 52 percent European-American, 29 percent African-American, 7 percent of Asian or Pacific Island descent, and 0.5 percent American Indian, Inuit, or Aleut; 24 percent are Spanish-speaking of various ethnic groups. That leaves a small percentage to other ethnic groupings — about 11.5 percent. But 11.5 percent of New York City's total population of 7,322,564 is more than enough to represent virtually every ethnic group on earth in America's largest city. And from steeplejacks to investment bankers, their jobs are as diverse as their family trees. Seven of America's ten largest banks are here, as is Wall Street, with the New York Stock Exchange and numerous related investment-banking firms. The World Trade Center, where multimillion-dollar deals take place daily, is here, too, in a pair of soaring towers that captured the nation's attention in 1993 when a terrorist bombing brought death and destruction to the towers and forced the temporary relocation of tens of thousands of office workers.

As the hub of an area covering parts of New York, New Jersey, and Connecticut (total metro population: 18 million), New York City is the geographic center of the nation's largest urban market for goods and services. Virtually every major ad agency has offices here, and the Associated Press and all the major networks have headquarters in New York. Dozens of book and magazine publishers are also here. Conventions and tourism are big business, too, with 20 million visitors flooding the Big Apple each year.

Top: West Street, New York City, 1883.
Bottom: Nassau Street Mall in modern New York City.

New York's credentials for its variety of experience, wealth of opportunity, and cultural diversity are endless. The borough of Queens is America's most racially diverse county. Four of New York's five boroughs are among the most racially diverse counties in the country. It's safe to say that New York City is a rich mix in a country that is itself a blend of a bit of everywhere.

Cycling at Venice Beach.

CHAPTER THREE

Los Angeles

Los Angeles began life in 1769, before the United States was more than a gleam in the eyes of East Coast patriots. It was founded by Gaspar de Portola, a Spaniard who was sent north from present-day Mexico to find suitable sites for religious missions. De Portola and his men traded gifts with Indians who were members of the Shoshone tribe. The visitors left the next morning, praising the area despite feeling three minor earthquakes overnight!

Mission San Gabriel was soon established, and the governor of California, Felipe de Neve, eventually recruited families of Mexicans, Africans, and American Indians to settle on the bank of what is now the Los Angeles River. Setting up missions like San Gabriel was the main reason for the European colonization of California. And as a way of getting the Indians to submit to the Spanish colonizers, these religious institutions generally proved quite effective — often with threats of eternal damnation.

The forty-four Spanish-speaking members of the settlement held a ceremony on September 4, 1781, giving the village a dramatic name: El Pueblo de Nuestra Señora la Reina de Los Angeles, or The Town of Our Lady the Queen of the Angels. The unusual name set the tone for the city from that day to this.

Yankee visitors were few and far between from the founding of the town to the early nineteenth century. Several Americans dropped anchor after sailing around South America, but the first U.S. citizen to reach the city by land was a tough fur trapper named Jedediah Smith, who arrived in 1826. At the time, the city belonged to Mexico, which had won independence from Spain in 1822. The new Mexican government thought enough of Los Angeles to change its status from *pueblo* to *ciudad* (from village to city) in 1836. Eleven years later, in 1847, the city became part of U.S. territory when Mexico surrendered California to the United States.

Water Fuels Farms and Ranches

Because only about 3,500 residents lived in the vast, usually dry area around Los Angeles, the nearby river provided enough fresh water for people and for cattle, too. *Zanjas*, or ditches, were dug in all directions to run fresh river water for crops and herds. Huge melons, bulbous squashes, and many other fruits and vegetables grew well in the irrigated soil. The 1849 gold rush near San Francisco made some Angelenos rich as they raised and shipped cattle north to feed hungry prospectors. All the while, twenty-eight-square-mile Los Angeles was evolving from a Mexican to an American city. By 1860, bullfighting was banned, and Los Angeles had its own baseball club.

Los Angeles and San Francisco could communicate with each other by 1860, thanks to a telegraph line that had been strung the 380 miles up the coast. During that same decade, an enterprising fellow named Phineas Banning noticed that Los Angeles did not really have a harbor. He also noticed that San Pedro, more than twenty miles south, could easily shelter anchored ships. Banning constructed the Los Angeles and San Pedro Railroad to haul goods between the sea and the city, and Los Angeles annexed a long, narrow corridor where the railroad ran so that the area would receive city services. That long, thin arm still exists and can be followed by driving south out of Los Angeles on Interstate Highway 110.

All the while, Los Angeles grew. California's first Chinese immigrant showed up in the mid-1800s, and by 1871 a mob of angry European-Americans had rioted, lynching twenty Chinese men because the Chinese were willing to work for lower wages than most other Americans would accept.

Other kinds of gatherings were created by a land boom occurring in the 1880s. These early land sales featured huge barbecues as ways to entice people onto the property being sold. Potential farmland was overrun with rabbits. To rid the land for planting, rifle-toting residents used rabbits trapped by snow fence for target practice.

There were one hundred thousand Angelenos by 1900, and five hundred thousand just twenty years later, when Los Angeles surpassed San Francisco as California's largest city. Mexicans saw prosperity in California and migrated north. Most crops were planted by machine but required hand picking, and so labor was needed to harvest strawberries, tomatoes, grapes, oranges, and other produce. Many kinds of jobs sprang up between harvests, and some Mexicans actually became well-to-do. Others, however, suffered discrimination, in part because some Angelenos illegally paid below-minimum wages, as they did to the Chinese in the nineteenth century and continue to do today. The impatience — and intolerance — that Anglos felt toward Latinos boiled over in 1943, when riots directed at young Mex-

This cartoon shows the mistreatment of early Chinese immigrants.

icans erupted. Today Mexican-Americans have become a highly visible and vital part of the fabric of Los Angeles' population, and most of them continue to live in the troubled neighborhoods of East Los Angeles.

Citrus to Go

In 1886, only a year after the first interstate rail line reached Los Angeles, a train loaded exclusively with fresh oranges left for the East Coast. Orange seeds had been brought from Europe by Spaniards years earlier and had always grown well in the warm, sunny climate. The demand for oranges proved to be incredible. Growers of various kinds of citrus decided to make their products more appealing than those from Florida or Texas by labeling them "Sunkist."

Everyone seemed promotion minded. To attract residents, suburban Pasadena created a celebration in the 1880s called the Tournament of Roses that has become a New Year's Day tradition.

As if the area weren't sufficiently blessed, a fellow named Edward Doheny took a second look at the bothersome tar that blackened the feet of bathers on the city's beaches. The gooey substance turned out to be oil, and Doheny began to successfully dig for it in 1892. By the late 1890s oil derricks had cropped up in numerous city neighborhoods, and in 1921 Royal Dutch Shell brought in a well on Signal Hill in southern Los Angeles County. That project proved to be part of the most productive oil field found in the United States.

Top: Migrant workers pick the orange crop in the 1890s.
Middle and bottom: Colorful labels for crates of citrus.

Louis B. Mayer

Louis Mayer was born half a world away from Los Angeles in the Russian town of Minsk in 1885. Yet no one did more to shape the image that became Hollywood and the motion-picture business.

Brought to Canada as a child, Mayer worked in his father's Massachusetts scrap-iron business from the age of fourteen. He saved his money and in 1907 opened a small movie theater. By 1918, he owned the largest theater chain in New England. But like other moviemakers, he didn't care for the unpredictable northern weather. And so, to ensure a steady supply of movies, Mayer moved to Hollywood and opened Louis B. Mayer Pictures. Six years and several mergers later, he was in charge of the giant film studio known as Metro-Goldwyn-Mayer, or MGM.

The movie mogul invented the star system in the 1930s and 1940s. He emphasized the glamor of actors and actresses, making sure that names such as Joan Crawford, Greta Garbo, Clark Gable, and Rudolf Valentino were displayed as prominently as the movie itself. The moviegoing public loved his lavish films, which included *Ben Hur* (1926), *Grand Hotel* (1932), *Dinner at Eight* (1933), and *The Good Earth* (1937).

For an hour or two each Saturday afternoon, this son of Russian Jews helped Americans forget the Great Depression by giving them wonderful, inexpensive entertainment. Louis Mayer handed over control of the studio to others in 1948, retired in 1951, and died an incredibly wealthy man in 1957.

Fair-weather Films

Drawn by the sun, the movies left New York for California. Moviemakers could go to bed at night confident that tomorrow's weather would allow them to shoot their project, which was often under tight deadlines and short of funds. The first film studio opened in Hollywood the same year Hollywood annexed itself to Los Angeles — in 1910. David Horsley's Nestor Film Company moved into what had been a tavern on Sunset Boulevard. Within the decade, the Vitagraph Company opened in Santa Monica, Universal began in North Hollywood, and Goldwyn started up in what would be Culver City. Many others followed. Together, they became the film industry, and the name Hollywood would become synonymous with moviemaking.

Movies became big business, and the heads of studios saw their names in the opening credits of pictures around the world. Many studio owners and early stars were Jewish, products of vaudeville and the East Coast entertainment business. Their

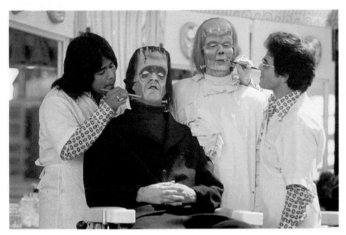

Top: Hollywood in the early 1940s.
Bottom: Make-up artists give two actors a new look.

work rewarded them in at least two ways: incredible wealth and the realization that they would be setting trends and dictating tastes of Americans for years. Names such as Darryl F. Zanuck, Louis Mayer, and Adolph Zukor were seen in darkened theaters by aspiring actors and actresses, scriptwriters, and directors. The legend fed itself, as studios hired dozens of publicity experts to crank out endless words and set up countless opportunities for the public to view stars under contract to the various studios.

One of the few studios within the city limits of Los Angeles itself was Twentieth Century-Fox. The city grew around the huge Fox studio, which fell deeply into debt after producing several box-office flops in the 1950s. The bosses at Fox solved the problem in a way that would make any Los Angeles real-estate magnate proud: they sold off part of their property as a housing development! Wrecking balls slammed into the false fronts of movie sets, and in their place arose the dream homes of middle-class Angelenos in a new area known since then as Century City.

Piping in Water — and Dreams

No one was of more importance to the growth of the Los Angeles area than an immigrant Irishman named William Mulholland. He arrived in Los Angeles in 1877 and was hired as a *zanjero* — one who shoveled water ditches to keep them flowing freely. Mulholland must have disliked the labor, because he studied and eventually became the chief engineer on the Owens Valley project. This scheme involved construction of a huge aqueduct running up and down the hills from the Owens Valley to the San Fernando Valley. By the end of 1912, the water had begun to flow, and, like a vampire, greater Los Angeles and its aqueducts soon sucked the liquid life out of Owens Valley and other rural spots.

An aggressive bunch soon took control of the city, selling winter-weary Midwesterners on the advantages of a warm climate, clean air, and oranges you could pick off your own backyard trees. The migration began, intensified during the Great Depression of the 1930s, and showed signs of weakening only in the 1980s. It was no accident that the first transcontinental airplane flight began in New York City and ended in Los Angeles — in nearby Pasadena, actually — in 1913. Indeed, California was seen by most Americans as the ultimate destination, a land where dreams could come true.

Growing Pains and Gains

One dream that briefly came true only to die a premature death in L.A. was that of mass transit. Before the automobile established itself on the West Coast, the big red Pacific Electric streetcars rumbled on tracks all over Los Angeles. Hardly ever profitable, the streetcars ran on tracks that were in public streets. Increasingly, cars stopping on the tracks prevented the streetcars from operating at maximum efficiency. With L.A. a prime marketing target for the auto industry, and with more and more families buying cars, city administrators were reluctant to prop up streetcar operations with public money. The last electric streetcar was retired in 1963.

The period spanning World War II and 1960 saw huge growth in L.A. By 1951, a transcontinental microwave system allowed television sets in Los Angeles and New York City to be tuned to the same program. The beloved Brooklyn Dodgers were lured in 1958 to Los Angeles by a fat checkbook and a new stadium. The Dodgers were a National League team that had staked its claim to baseball history by breaking major league baseball's color line with the signing of African-American superstar Jackie Robinson in the 1940s. The team also had a tradition of losing the World Series to the cross-town and American League rival New York Yankees. By 1963, the transplanted Dodgers were able to sweep the Yankees in the Series, four games to none. A few years later, Los Angeles got a second team — the expansion Angels, who eventually moved to neighboring Anaheim. Los Angeles had joined New York and Chicago as the only cities supporting more than one major league baseball team.

Rioting, looting, and arson hit south-central Los Angeles in late April and early May of 1992 after an all-white, suburban jury found four Los Angeles policemen innocent in the beating of Black motorist Rodney King. The incident, which took place in 1991, was videotaped by a bystander. That tape was the prosecution's key piece of evidence in the trial. When Black Los Angeles learned of the verdict, many attacked white- and Korean-owned stores — and individuals. A total of 4,900 Marines, Army, and National

Signs, iron bars, and a poster of Malcolm X bear witness to rioting in 1992.

Guard troops eventually restored order after a dusk-to-dawn curfew was ignored. More than fifty persons died in the unrest in a city where many African-Americans, homosexuals, young people, and Mexican-Americans had grown suspicious of white police officers. Mayor Tom Bradley, himself African-American, criticized both the verdict of the jury and the lawlessness that followed.

The wrath aimed at Koreans was more complex. Since the 1950s Koreans have migrated to the United States, especially to its larger, coastal cities. They brought money to purchase and operate grocery, convenience, or other kinds of stores, often in mostly African-American neighborhoods. Some Blacks have watched these comparative newcomers succeed, and they believe in some cases that Korean success is connected to racism — preferential treatment for Koreans and discrimination against Blacks, whose history in America, after all, goes back for centuries. Koreatown merchants armed themselves during the King riot and later claimed that police were slow in coming to their aid.

The suffering of every ethnic group in America has at one time or another been mirrored by their experiences in L.A. Japanese-Americans numbered about forty thousand in the area when World War II began. Most were farmers who were moved away from the coast into internment camps after President Franklin D. Roosevelt signed an executive order in 1942. The federal government feared these Americans would cooperate with the enemy at the time, though nothing but their ancestry could ever be raised to substantiate such fears. Many of the Nisei, or second-generation Japanese-Americans, who had been interred in the camps returned to Los Angeles, frequently as professionals. The bitter knowledge that overnight their government had turned them into second-class citizens has never left them.

Who Lives in Los Angeles?

Because they're always on the move, Angelenos are tough to pin down. But a recent survey shows the city with a population of 3,485,398 in a sprawling metropolitan area of more than 14.5 million. In the city, some 53 percent of these highly mobile people are European-American, 14 percent African-American, 10 percent of Asian or Pacific Island descent, about 0.5 percent American Indian, Inuit, or Aleut, and the remainder of other, unspecified ethnic groupings. About 40 percent are Hispanics of varied ethnic groups.

The city is bounded on the west by the Pacific Ocean. Several mountains cut through the metropolitan area at various angles. Among them are the

Top: A mural adorns a building at Venice Beach.
Middle: Melrose Avenue and The Burger That Ate L.A.
Bottom: Olvera Street.

Santa Monica and San Gabriel Mountains and the Dominguez and Puente Hills. The mountains hold in carbon monoxide and other gases, resulting in frequent, thick layers of smog. The air can become a danger to persons with heart and lung problems, but the smog can also disappear in minutes if a brisk, eastern Santa Anna wind blows in. Other hazards of life in Los Angeles include earthquakes, mudslides, and forest fires, one of which was so vigorous that it leapt over an entire freeway in the late 1960s!

Los Angeles has depended on defense business for some time. But the city's economy is diverse, with manufacturing, retailing, oil-refining, and finance responsible for huge payrolls. Manufactured goods include electrical equipment, machinery, iron, pottery, glassware, and chemicals. L.A. is, of course, the film capital of the world, with every major American movie studio in the metropolitan area. A movie may cost millions to make, but it can earn that much in a single weekend as copies are shown all over North America.

A Midwesterner moved to the Los Angeles area, succeeded at his work, and returned to the Midwest after almost twenty years of life in Southern California. He departed the West Coast because he grew tired of fighting freeway traffic four hours in each direction, just for a meeting that lasted ninety minutes or less! Yet the former Californian speaks well of the people he knew in the West.

"People in Los Angeles feel anything is possible," he recalls. "They look at every problem as if it can be solved. That's a great attitude, one you just don't find many other places." On the other hand, he believes that many Angelenos "are trying to convince themselves that Los Angeles is the great place to live that it once was, a long time ago."

Chicago's modern skyline provides a stunning backdrop to a crowded lake shore concert.

CHAPTER FOUR

Chicago

The young American had seen no one from the United States and heard nothing about his hometown of Chicago for weeks. He was vacationing half a world away from the United States in Thailand. Yet it seemed that whenever he told Thais where he was from, he received the same reaction: the strangers acted as if they were holding submachine guns and yelled something like, "You Chicago tough guy? Ratatatatatatat!" Obviously, Chicago's longtime reputation as a city filled with mobsters was still alive.

When Chicago's many accomplishments are added up, the assumption about gangsters is unfair. The city, for example, is the home of the skyscraper, which was developed by a group known together as the Chicago School of Architecture. Their influence in the late nineteenth century was so important that the average Chicago resident today can talk knowledgeably about cornices and ramparts and other facets of building design. Homes designed by Frank Lloyd Wright, America's most famous architect, dot the suburbs.

A City of Superlatives

The Chicago School. Chicago Style. From architecture to literature, from pizza to hot dogs to music, *Chicago* is the word many use to describe what is newest, most progressive, or tastiest. In political science, the Chicago School refers to the psychological study of politics that became popular in the Midwest's largest city in the 1920s. About the same time, along came Chicago Style, a way of improvising jazz music that represented the first attempt by white musicians to introduce jazz as it came up the Mississippi River from New Orleans to blend with their own music.

From about 1912 to 1925 came Chicago's literary renaissance. Sherwood Anderson, Theodore Dreiser, Edgar Lee Masters, Carl Sandburg, and others became popular by depicting big city life as it really was. Later writers with Chicago connections, those whose words would cover the years of World War II and afterward, include Saul Bellow, James Farrell, and Ben Hecht. These writers also brought to life a Chicago that could be gritty, immoral, wide open.

The city has fifty-eight colleges and two hundred technical schools, and the University of Chicago stands as one of America's great beacons to

Chicago after the fire of 1871.

scholars. Among the nation's top schools before World War II, only Chicago — and Columbia University in New York City — refused to put quotas on the number of Jewish students admitted. Consequently, the university on Lake Michigan's south shore lured many superior students without regard to their ethnic background. In 1937 the school dropped high school credits as a basis for admission and has consistently emphasized the importance of adult education.

Tragedy, Tumult, and Turmoil

Yet for all its accomplishments, the city knows tragedy, controversy, and hardship. The Chicago Fire, blamed on a fictitious cow kicking over a lantern, burned October 8-11, 1871. There was no loss of life, but the cost was estimated at $196 million. In 1915, a cruise ship, the *Eastland*, tipped over in Lake Michigan when passengers ran from one rail to the other. The capsized boat took 812 persons to a watery grave.

The worst single-plane air disaster in U.S. history took place in 1979 after an engine fell off an American Airlines DC-10 passenger jet seconds after takeoff from O'Hare Airport. The crash killed 275 passengers. And in 1992, water from the Chicago River flooded the basements of many large buildings, causing millions of dollars in damage.

Despite the unfair "tough-guy" treatment of our visitor to Thailand, there is some truth to the city's reputation as a crime den. Prohibition, which made the consumption of alcoholic beverages illegal in the United States from 1917 to 1933, was a bonanza for organized crime. Chicago's criminals made millions smuggling liquor into the country from Canada and elsewhere. They

Gangster Al Capone.

were good at it, but they became greedy. So it was no surprise on February 14, 1929, when gangsters, disguised as police, killed seven of their rivals in a Near North Side garage in the "St. Valentine's Day Massacre."

The authorities could never catch the city's most famous crook, Al Capone, bootlegging liquor or making money from gambling or prostitution. So federal authorities nabbed him in 1931 for failing to pay taxes on his ill-gotten fortune. Federal officials were needed, because many local police officers and politicians had been paid off by his mob.

Chicago is a city of neighborhoods that are tightly knit and often resistant to outside influences. Perhaps because race and ethnicity have long played a major role in the city's politics, relations among Chicago's ethnic groups have not always been ideal. Following World War I, for example, large numbers of African-Americans from the south migrated to Chicago, so that the city's African-

American population grew from 44,000 in 1910 to nearly 110,000 by 1920. On the afternoon of July 27, 1919, an African-American boy cooling off in Lake Michigan swam into a white area and was hit with stones and drowned. Police refused to arrest a white man identified by onshore Blacks as causing the boy's death, and an angry crowd of African-Americans gathered on the South Side beach. Rumors, mob rule, and violence swept the city for thirteen days, leaving 38 persons dead, 537 injured, and a thousand Black families homeless.

Ironically, Chicago began peacefully enough. Like the sites of many American cities east of the Mississippi River, Chicago's first European visitors were French. In this case, the foreigners were French priests, Louis Joliet and Jacques Marquette. The two were impressed in 1673 with what would one day be called the Chicago River because it emptied into Lake Michigan yet could be traveled westward virtually to the Mississippi River. Not that the location on the southwest corner of Lake Michigan was great. The area was made up mostly of mud flats, mosquitoes infested the area in warm weather, and the rutted or soupy mud made travel difficult virtually any time of the year.

"The Father of Chicago" and the Making of a City

The first non-Indian settler in the place that would become Chicago was a Black man — Jean-Baptist Point du Sable, the son of a Quebec merchant father and a Black Haitian mother. Du Sable came to the area in 1770 at the age of about twenty. He settled at the mouth of the Chicago River, married

Jane Addams and Hull House

Settlement houses were an English idea. They were conceived as places for the poor to turn to in times of need. They were also places where the less fortunate could socialize in a healthy atmosphere. America's most famous settlement house was Chicago's Hull House. It was founded by a well-educated rural Illinois woman, Jane Addams.

Addams graduated from college and attended medical school for two years in the 1880s before her health failed. She recovered by traveling to Europe, where she visited a settlement house in a London industrial district. Returning to the United States, she and a friend, Ellen Gates Starr, decided to create a settlement house in Chicago.

The two women acquired a big house built in 1856 by a man named Hull. The home was in a thickly settled, working-class neighborhood; it opened as Hull House in 1889. Because the two tirelessly sought donations and because Hull House offered exactly the kinds of services so desperately needed by recent immigrants and big-city poor people, it grew. In time, Hull House came to include thirteen different buildings, plus a camp near Lake Geneva, Wisconsin.

Hull House had everything from a day-care center to a gymnasium, from a school offering basic English to a school that provided college-level training. Hull House Players, a theater group, became known for its dramatic productions. The facility also featured a laboratory where future social workers received training.

Jane Addams saw what was wrong with the lives of big-city poor people and became an intense reformer. She lobbied for regulation of juvenile courts, for housing safety, for the eight-hour workday for women, for factory safety and health inspections, and for justice for immigrants and African-Americans. In 1910 she was elected first woman president of the National Conference of Social Work.

a Potawatomi woman, and began to build a successful trading business. His loyalty to France and then America eventually caused his arrest by the British, who held him prisoner at a Michigan outpost. Du Sable was released at the end of the Revolutionary War and returned to Chicago. He prospered, dealing in furs and grain and reinforcing the notion that Chicago was an important shipping and trading site.

But as important as Chicago was becoming, at the time it wasn't necessarily safe — at least not to others who came to settle and exploit its resources. Fort Dearborn, a U.S. Army post, was erected on the river but was destroyed by Indians in 1812. Rebuilt four years later, the post protected but a few cabins and shacks, and by the time Illinois became a state in 1818, several sites elsewhere in the state were growing much faster than Chicago. But that changed after 1825, the year the Erie Canal was completed. As a result, the fastest way west for land-hungry eastern settlers became the canal and then a boat to the Great Lakes that docked in Chicago.

Chicago quickly became a crucial spot for the settlers to stock up on provisions before striking out for their new land. Commerce fed upon this success, as large storage facilities were built to hold supplies and to keep grain and other goods shipped east after the pioneers stepped off the boats that had brought them to Illinois. Because the city continued to be so low lying, local government decided to raise the entire site three feet! This didn't help drainage, which continued to be poor in this very flat city. But it seemed to make sense at a time when Chicago was booming and any civic suggestion was seriously considered.

A Strategic Location

Throughout the nineteenth century, many events came together to further increase the city's importance. The federal government opened a regional land office in the city; canals and rivers were connected in 1848 to link the Great Lakes and the Mississippi River; and the first railroad line reached Chicago in 1852.

In an incredibly short period of time — in fact, before the Civil War began — Chicago had become the nation's rail center. By 1869, it was the hub of a rail route that stretched from one coast to the other. By the end of the century, a rail map of the United States looked as if every road in existence passed through the Windy City.

Chicago was in the right place at the right time for the Industrial Revolution, which really began in England about 1815 and spread to America and elsewhere. The city was just asserting itself as a supplier to agriculture when several different Midwestern inventors came up with mechanized farm machinery. The most well known was the McCormick reaper, made in Chicago. Other implements that moved farming from the nineteenth to the twentieth century included the John Deere tractor, made in western Illinois, and Case and Allis-Chalmers tractors, created between Chicago and Milwaukee in nearby southeast Wisconsin. From 1860 to 1914, the city's population increased from 110,000 to 2 million.

An early slaughter-house.

"Hog Butcher to the World" and Multicultural Magnet

Farm surpluses grew incredibly, causing poet Carl Sandburg to accurately call Chicago the "hog butcher to the world." Jobs related in some way to agriculture were widely available, if not always glamorous. Southern Blacks, lured by higher wages, took many of the dirty and unattractive jobs in slaughterhouses, foundries, and steel mills. These African-Americans traveled a familiar road — U.S. Highway 61 — north along the Mississippi River to tenement housing, long working hours, and discrimination. They brought with them the same sweet blues music that echoed across cotton fields a thousand miles south. That sound has been electrified with hot guitars and sophisticated amplifiers, and it is today a popular source of entertainment in Chicago clubs.

In addition to Chicago's African-American population, the city's neighborhoods are home to a variety of other ethnic groupings, no two of which came to Chicago at the same time or for the same reasons. Among these groups, the following are notable for their role in shaping the city's character and personality:

Chicago's Chinatown.

The first Chinese came to Chicago, not from China but from America's West Coast. They came in 1860, deciding to move east because of anti-Chinese sentiment in California. The first area to be called Chinatown was so named in 1880 and lasted until 1972, when it was razed for the construction of a jail. The second Chinatown was located on the city's Near South Side in an old Italian neighborhood. A third Chinatown, made up in part of various Southeast Asians and ethnic Chinese who fled Vietnam in 1975, is known as "Little Saigon." It is on the city's north side.

Chicago's first Puerto Ricans showed up in 1893 and won medals for their coffee and tobacco at the Columbian Exposition, an early world's fair. They enjoyed the city and stayed. Among the offspring of the first islanders was U.A. Sanavria. Sanavria, while employed by the Hearst newspaper chain, invented a working TV set in 1930. In contrast to Chicago's urban, educated Puerto Ricans, the island's country people began to arrive after World War II. Among the first to show up were cigar makers, who could find work in almost any big U.S. city at the time.

Chicago's Polish-Americans, an ethnic force in a city with many Eastern European neighborhoods, hoped their country would be free following the defeat of Nazi Germany in World War II. But their hopes were dashed by the spread of Soviet-style communism. Poles who survived the war and postwar periods in detention camps came to Chicago in large numbers as displaced persons. The men secured jobs making steel on the South Side and in nearby northwest Indiana. Their children — and grandchildren — today are aldermen, attorneys, real estate brokers, and physicians. Wicker Park, a West Side neighborhood where pre-World War I Polish businesspersons built big houses after being excluded from lakefront property, underwent extensive renewal in the 1970s.

Politics as Usual and the Last Big-City Boss

Some say the city grew not because of city government but despite it. "Chicago ain't ready for reform," a political hack was once quoted as saying. Typically, the city was headed by a Democratic mayor who worked with aldermen, also usually Democrats. These aldermen each represented a district that was broken down into wards, which were really neighborhoods. When a ward resident wanted a pothole filled or a streetlight replaced, he or she called the alderman's assistants, who passed the request on up to the alderman, who would see to it that some kind of city crew made the repair. In exchange, that ward owed him its vote. The system wasn't pretty, but it worked.

With the death of the powerful Mayor Richard J. Daley in 1976, such machine politics were dealt a mortal blow. Daley was the last of the traditional big-city political bosses, a short, tough Irishman who attracted business and backed urban renewal but did little to promote racial harmony or end redlining, which is the practice of discriminating among lenders who buy and sell houses in changing or minority neighborhoods. As mayor from 1955 until his death in 1976, Daley came to be the symbol of all that was good and bad in Chicago. Alliances in Chicago politics have often been forged along racial and ethnic — as well as party — lines, and after terms by Michael Bilandic and Jane Byrne following Daley's death, the office was won by an African-American, the late Harold Washington. The election of Washington in 1983 was a historic event in local and national big-city politics. A man of great personal charisma and dedication to reform, Washington was revered by many. His term was marked by bitter clashes with white city council members, many of them members of his own party. He died in office in 1987 and was succeeded by Dick Daley, the late mayor's son, after Black voters split into different factions and failed to unite behind a single candidate.

National and local politics and dissent clashed in Chicago in 1968. Antiwar demonstrators, the counterculture, and chaos-loving Yippies demonstrated during the Democratic National Convention. Mayor Daley, a man who favored U.S. participation in the Vietnam War and disliked disruptions, ordered police to end the protests. The police battered everyone from the most slovenly activist to the most tidy priest, causing a riot that spilled into the headquarters of at least one major Democratic presidential candidate. The tumult was shown on network TV and gave the city a reputation it took years to overcome.

Many People, Much to Do

According to one recent survey, about 45 percent of Chicago's present population is European-American and 40 percent is African-American. People of Asian or Pacific Island descent total just under 4 percent, while American Indians, Inuits, and Aleuts total under 1 percent. The remainder represent a variety of other ethnic groupings; Spanish-speaking residents of all ethnic groups account for 20 percent of the population. Speaking of population, Chicago totals 2,783,726 and boasts a metropolitan population of over 8,065,633 in a tri-state area that covers parts of Illinois, Indiana, and Wisconsin. Chicago keeps these people busy with a variety of business and industry. If one kind of work is slow, another will be booming. There are ten thousand factories producing candy, frozen foods, furniture, housewares, machinery, petroleum products, and railroad equipment.

Top: Old Town is thick with majestic buildings. *Bottom:* Neon lights up a moving walkway in Chicago's O'Hare Airport.

The city is remarkable in so many ways. It is devoted to sports, being one of only three cities (New York and Los Angeles are the other two) capable of supporting two major-league baseball teams. It is a center for advertising and publishing, it has the world's busiest airport, and virtually every trucking firm worthy of the name has facilities in or near the city. Because of its central location, Japanese firms often locate their U.S. headquarters in or near the city. Chicago often is the next stop for cultural events from either New York or Los Angeles (the only U.S. cities with populations greater than Chicago's), and many musical and theatrical groups begin in Chicago and go on to national and international success. The metropolitan area continues to be a desirable place to live, in part because of its superior public-transit system. Insulated from extreme economic swings and with a stable population, Chicago will long be the most formidable and influential city in the Midwest.

Detroit's Renaissance Center by night.

CHAPTER FIVE

Detroit

The shop owner could not believe his eyes. Two African-American men, people who were occasional customers, had just thrown bricks through his front window. What was going on? It was 1943, and the clothing merchant, who was white and Jewish, was the target of resentment — even though, like the Blacks, he was a member of a minority group. These men were showing their frustration toward anyone who was white. After all, there were thousands of jobs in defense factories, and many African-Americans had been shut out in their repeated attempts to find work. Yet barely literate whites from Kentucky, West Virginia, and elsewhere in Appalachia continued to come to Detroit, and they were hired. Hence, the bricks.

That episode was part of a huge riot that began on June 21, 1943, in a city where rioting has occurred too often. It resulted in seven hundred injuries and thirty-four deaths. Most of the dead and injured were African-Americans, some of whom had disobeyed the law, all of whom had been unlucky enough to be in the wrong place at the wrong time. Compared to the Detroit riot, a riot in New York's Harlem the same year was barely a disagreement. In an industrial town whose fortunes rise and fall with the nation's economy, Detroit's minorities have suffered even more than most. And perhaps because African-Americans have for so long played such a large role in the Detroit scene, they seldom conceal their feelings.

Fort Ponchartrain du Detroit

In contrast to such clashes, the first European found the area he would name Detroit a thinly populated, pleasant, and peaceful place. Visited in 1701 by French trader Antoine de la Mothe Cadillac, the site was bounded by what is now known as the Detroit River, which connects Lake Erie with Lake St. Clair and Lake Huron. Ontario, today Canada's most populous province, is just across the river. Cadillac arrived by boat, and boats and shipping have played major parts in the city's history ever since.

Cadillac constructed a fort and named it Ponchartrain du Detroit (Ponchartrain "of the strait"). Ponchartrain was an official in the court of Louis XIV, the French king at the time. Cadillac served as the area's governor before

Chief Pontiac.

being sent to Louisiana in 1710. The site (it couldn't yet be called a city) was transferred to the British in 1760. Local Ottawa Indians viewed the deal as yet one more instance of European encroachment on Indian land. Under Chief Pontiac, the Ottawa fought the British for control of their land, but after a long and bitter battle, the British prevailed.

Like all British lands west of the Allegheny Mountains, the fort came into U.S. hands following the American Revolution. But British soldiers did not abandon the settlement. Instead, they encouraged Indians in the area to attack settlers as they migrated west. Eventually, the Indians were subdued and U.S. soldiers in 1796 took control of the fort. Detroit was handed back and forth one more time, in the War of 1812. The fort was surrendered to the British without a fight in 1812, and they held it until 1813. But the British abandoned it after Oliver Hazard Perry defeated them in a naval battle on Lake Erie. Perry's victory had broken the Indian-British alliance.

A Temporary Capital City

Small though it may have been, Detroit was one of the few fortified sites in the Michigan Territory. So it proved to be a wise choice as the capital, from 1805 to 1837, of the territory made up of today's states of Michigan, Wisconsin, and part of Minnesota. In the first year as a territorial seat, 1805, log homes and buildings were wiped out by a fire; in fact, the entire settlement was leveled. But by 1810, a census counted 1,650 permanent, hardy residents. Among the first settlers were Moravian teachers and German-Czech Protestants, who cut a trail out of Detroit and built homes in what would become nearby Mt. Clemens, Michigan.

The city received a real shot in the arm in 1818 when regular steamboat service began between Buffalo and Detroit. This was the first of several passenger and freight services that opened up the lands bordering the central and western Great Lakes. Detroit became a business center as grain and lumber were stockpiled there for shipment and shipbuilding and machinery construction began in earnest. This early work, together with skilled employees, laid a solid foundation for Detroit to take the lead in the automobile industry. Once rails were laid into and out of the city, grain bound for Europe was hauled to Detroit for shipping overseas.

Detroit's proximity to Canada made it an important way station for Blacks using the Underground Railroad to escape slavery.

The Underground Railroad

The first African-Americans to visit Detroit may have been slaves who escaped to freedom via the Underground Railroad. Neither beneath the ground nor a railroad, the term applies to whites and freed Blacks who bravely defied the Fugitive Slave Acts before the Civil War to smuggle slaves to freedom in the North or into Canada, where slave hunters dared not go. The Detroit station was a critical stop for Blacks who chose to enter Canada.

Estimates of the number of slaves who escaped range from forty thousand to one hundred thousand, though only a fraction of them ever passed through Detroit. Those who did come through Detroit wanted their children to have an education. In 1869, with the pressures of Civil War Reconstruction and the Bill of Rights, plus an activist U.S. Supreme Court, the city admitted "colored children" to its public schools. Prior to this admission, separate schools had been maintained. School officials decided African-American children would be "on perfectly equal terms with all others."

Post-Civil War Boom Times

Following the Civil War, the northern Midwest forests were attacked in earnest by thousands of lumberjacks. Stands of white pine throughout Michigan, Wisconsin, and Minnesota were dropped and then floated to mills, primarily for housing construction. Detroit became a lumber center, with several men becoming millionaires from the quality and quantity of the tree harvest. At the same time, the city experienced a publishing boom, producing newspapers and magazines in a frenzy that would last past 1900.

Detroit was becoming heavily industrialized, too, and had publications for industrialists such as *The Mechanic & Inventor* beginning in 1867 and *The Scientific Manufacturer*, from 1873. A group of Jesuit priests responded to educational needs by founding the University of Detroit in 1877. That same year, Detroit's first telephone was installed. Three years later, the Detroit Council of Trades and Labor Unions was formed. And by 1890, the American Federation of Labor held its national convention in Detroit, featuring union pioneer Samuel Gompers. When the automobile industry began to construct cars in quantity early in the twentieth century, Detroit responded.

Fords and Cadillacs —
Good Times and Bad

The first Cadillac was produced in 1902, ten years after the first Ford. And then, on October 1, 1908, carmaker Henry Ford stunned the world when he introduced a massed-produced car, fresh from a Detroit assembly line, for $850. Cars prior to this had been handmade one at a time and were priced out of reach of all but the wealthiest families. The car would change America's

Historic Detroit, as seen from the Canadian shore.

Top: Autoworkers assemble a car in the 1930s.
Bottom: Finished cars at a General Motors plant in the 1940s.

landscape, give it the world's best roads, and provide employment for Detroit-area residents for decades. Ford knew that, unless the masses were making decent wages, his plans to build a mass-produced car would be doomed. He raised wages of assemblers in 1914 from $2.40 for a nine-hour day to $5.00 for an eight-hour day. Just over twenty years later, in 1937, unionized auto workers won their first big contracts.

As cars became more popular, more and better roadways were needed. A new bridge between Detroit and its neighbor across the river, Windsor, Ontario, was dedicated in 1929. In 1927, Ford brought out the hugely successful Model A, and by 1931, despite the Great Depression, Henry Ford had constructed 20 million vehicles. Detroiters became more socially conscious as they had less money. In 1933, a rally at the armory to protest German persecution of its Jewish minority population drew an estimated ten thousand persons. Ironically, Detroit's African-American population wasn't yet seen as an ill-treated minority.

There was little to buoy residents during the hard '30s — except for pro sports. In 1934 the Detroit Tigers won the American League championship for the first time in twenty-five years and went on to win the World Series. In 1935, the Detroit Lions won the professional football title, and in 1936 the Detroit Red Wings hockey team captured the Stanley Cup. Meanwhile, Joe Louis, an African-American fighter, was making Detroiters proud as he knocked out virtually every opponent he faced en route to the world heavyweight boxing championship.

The large number of unemployed people called for new ways of thinking and planning in the city, and in 1938 the first tenants moved into the Brewster and Parkside public-housing projects. These apartments were intended for people who did not have enough money to buy or rent anywhere else. Unfortunately, Blacks and whites clashed in 1942 at another housing project, this one called Sojourner Truth. Part of the problem — economics — was solved by the Chrysler Corporation, which in 1940 began to build a $20 million factory that would produce army tanks. Many of the defense workers hired would be laid-off union members from the car industry.

Union Successes

The United Auto Workers (UAW) were at one time the largest and most successful labor union in the country. The union's rise and fall mirrors the city where it began. Unions became a significant part of manufacturing about

1930, when the Great Depression began. Workers wanted fair treatment, better pay, and improved working conditions. They also wanted layoffs, which occurred throughout the 1930s, to be based on seniority. In other words, they wanted the workers who had been at a plant the longest to be the *last* ones laid off.

Union membership peaked as a percentage of the work force in 1945, when 35 percent of hourly workers nationwide were union members. That figure is 16 percent today, with not all auto assembly plants unionized. That's especially true in states such as Tennessee, where there is no strong union feeling or tradition. The United Auto Workers today has a million members and also represents persons employed in the aerospace and farm implement businesses. Despite the trends away from large union memberships, the UAW can point with pride to an agreement with General Motors in 1948 that tied hourly wages to the cost of living. It can take credit, too, for auto assembly line hourly wages rising from $.76 in 1936 to $5.23 in 1972.

After the War — The City's Ups and Downs

One of the first projects following World War II was the attempt to curb blight, or deterioration, in the inner city. Conceived by the city's housing commission, the "Detroit Plan" sought to prevent Detroit's becoming an entire city of public housing. The plan was to work closely with private businesses to tear down old buildings and build new ones. The plan was a noble idea, but it counted on the downtown business district remaining strong. In Detroit as everywhere else, the use of cars led to the construction of outlying shopping centers, and downtown commercial areas decayed.

A partial answer has been a twenty-three-acre, $100 million redevelopment project, launched in 1959, that includes hotels, apartment houses, and shopping. To lure tourists more recently, the city has for the last several years staged an automobile race through downtown Detroit's temporarily closed-off

Joe Louis, the "Brown Bomber"

Joe Louis held the world's heavyweight boxing championship for twelve years, from 1937 to 1949. Although he was born in Alabama and his birth certificate says he is Joseph Louis Barrows, he's known to sports fans as Detroit's Joe Louis.

Louis's family migrated to Michigan, where job possibilities were better than in the South. Joe began his boxing career at the age of twenty in 1934, winning the U.S. Amateur Athletic Union 175-pound championship and a Golden Gloves title. His first professional fight took place just weeks later. Within a year he had knocked out Primo Carnera, the first of six previous or subsequent heavyweight champions who would challenge him.

The tall, strong African-American man was soft-spoken and gentle. Many whites came to boxing matches hoping he would get his block knocked off. They departed in awe of his skill and power and impressed by his modesty and pleasant disposition. In a 1938 championship match with racial and political overtones, Louis knocked out the German Max Schmeling in the first round of their fight. Schmeling had beaten Louis earlier in a nontitle bout.

Louis was willing to fight anyone. He also was willing to serve in World War II from 1942 to 1945, a move that shortened his career, which actually reached its peak during the period 1939-1942. In a six-month stretch in 1941, for example, he defended his title seven times. Following retirement with a record that included only three losses in hundreds of fights, Louis stayed busy making personal appearances. Both his heavyweight reign and his popularity have often been compared to those of Muhammad Ali.

The "Brown Bomber," as he was affectionately nicknamed, died in Las Vegas in 1981 at the age of 66.

streets. The problem of inner-city decay is one that Detroit has been combating for longer than most of its residents have been alive.

A number of women assumed supervisory roles during World War II, and by 1949 a woman, Mary V. Beck, took her seat on the city council. In 1973 State Senator Coleman A. Young, an African-American, was elected mayor of the city. His election came two years after a federal judge decided that Detroit and Detroit suburban schools were segregated and that they must be immediately integrated. Busing, which was unpopular with many people in the city and the suburbs alike, was used to balance the racial makeup of public schools. Earlier, in 1967, Blacks had tried unsuccessfully to boycott schools, calling them racist and unjust.

The city did not escape the turbulence of the 1960s. In fact, in 1967 and 1968, the country's most costly and intense rioting took place in the Motor City. Approximately fourteen hundred U.S. Army paratroops, some back from duty in Vietnam, found themselves the targets of angry Blacks. The resentment didn't end overnight. In 1969, a policeman was killed and another wounded by African separatists meeting at a West Side Baptist church. Relations between the police and Detroit's African-American community have been poor for some time, as a National Association for the Advancement of Colored People (NAACP) complaint in 1964 shows. And if the 1992 fatal beating of a Black motorist by five Detroit patrolmen is an indication, there is still a long way to go.

A Positive of Note — Motown Records

As in most cities, Detroit's struggle to stay on top of its troubles has produced its share of success as well as woe. One of the most fascinating success stories anywhere is that of Berry Gordy, an African-American auto worker who realized in the late 1950s that he could hear better voices in a Detroit church or street corner than he could tune in on his radio. Gordy started with a modest sound studio and auditioned young performers who became Diana Ross and the Supremes, Smoky Robinson and the Miracles, Martha and the Vandellas, Aretha Franklin, the Four Tops, the Temptations, and more. By the mid-1960s, Berry Gordy's Motown Records had taken command of Top 40 radio everywhere. And it happened without much of a bankroll and with the immense array of talented singers and songwriters from inner-city Detroit.

Who Lives in Detroit Today?

According to a 1990 survey, about three out of every four people in Detroit, or 75 percent, are African-American. About 22 percent of the population is European-American; less than 1 percent is of Asian or Pacific Island descent; about 0.5 percent is American Indian, Inuit, or Aleut; and the remaining 1.5 percent comes from various other ethnic groups. Spanish-speaking persons of any ethnic background amount to less than 3 percent of the population. Despite so few significant numbers other than whites and Blacks, several interesting ethnic groups have settled in the city's metropolitan area. Appalachian whites flocked to the city by the hundreds during World War II and

A Motown "45" offered a song on each side and sold for about one dollar in the 1960s.

spread throughout the metropolitan area. In contrast, Albanian Muslims have established a small community centered around a mosque in a Detroit suburb. There are also numerous Muslims from various Arab lands. The city's population, which is declining, is 1,027,974. The total population of the metropolitan area is 4,665,236.

Other important ethnic groups include more than sixty thousand Jews, many of whom came to Detroit from Eastern Europe after World War I. They were fed up with ineffective governments, with conflicts among political factions, and with the continued hostility of their German, Polish, Russian, and Ukrainian neighbors. Like Jews in many large U.S. cities in the early 1920s, many turned to trade, dealing in such exotic-seeming lines as rags and scrap metal. The Detroit clothing merchant whose windows were smashed in 1943 may well have been a son of these first-generation Americans.

A City of Losses and Gains

Detroit lost almost 200,000 persons, or about 14 percent of its population, during the period 1980-90. One of the reasons for the decline is the reduced number of jobs in the automobile industry. For at least twenty-five years, Japanese automakers have sent increasing numbers of cars to the United States. Popular at first because of their superior quality, the cars now have dealerships all across North America. More important, some of the vehicles are being produced in the United States. Companies such as Honda, Mazda, Mitsubishi, Nissan, Subaru, and Toyota have either built their own assembly plants or purchased existing facilities. A Mazda, for example, may have been assembled in a plant near Detroit, with three-fourths of its parts made in the U.S.A.

Detroit remains an important source for automobiles and parts, though U.S. automakers in recent years have taken jobs out of Detroit as they use lower-priced workers in the South, in Mexico, and elsewhere. The city still produces machine tools, engines, airplane parts, military devices, and plastics. The Port of Detroit is one of the five busiest in the U.S., since the Detroit River opens onto Lake Erie, which is connected to the St. Lawrence River, which in turn meets the Atlantic Ocean.

Detroit's up-and-down fortunes have been closely linked to those of larger economic and industrial trends. And yet business and industry have long been drawn to Detroit by its strategic location, solid industrial base, and powerful work force. Detroit has also attracted visitors with its four big-league sports teams, such long-standing cultural attractions as the Institute of Arts, which features murals by noted Mexican artist Diego Rivera depicting Detroit industry and labor, and such draws as the Renaissance Center — which includes many hotel rooms and meeting facilities, plus twenty-eight restaurants and numerous shops. This is a city that must be respected for the life it has made for itself out of the grittiness and energy of urban America.

The Supremes (top) and the Temptations were two of many groups to hit it big on the Motown label.

Downtown San Francisco forms the backdrop for well-kept Victorian homes.

A Multicultural Portrait of Life in the Cities

CHAPTER SIX

San Francisco

An off-duty city police officer, a member of the infamous Hell's Angels motorcycle gang, an African-American computer engineer, and a gay teacher meet and share common ground in very few places. One of them is at the parts counter of Perkins Harley-Davidson, the oldest such motorcycle dealership in continuous existence and one of hundreds of minor landmarks in San Francisco, a city so exotic that one of its newspaper columnists called it "Baghdad by the Bay."

Few cities anywhere have had a more uproarious history. The first European to view what is among the most beautiful and dramatic settings for any city ever — a spacious bay, the golden hills, and the sun and fog — was Gaspar de Portola. If that name sounds familiar, it's because he also is credited with being the first non-native to explore the area that is today's Los Angeles. De Portola and his party stood atop a hill and took in the Bay area in 1775, several years after explorers such as Juan Rodríguez Cabrillo and Sir Francis Drake sailed past the entrance to the bay without pausing to look around.

A Point of U.S.-Mexican Rivalry

Mexican settlers took up Bay-area residence in 1776 near the location today of the Golden Gate Bridge — where the Bay and the Pacific Ocean meet. Lieutenant José Joaquin Moraga established an army post, the Presidio, which is in use by the United States Army today, while the Rev. Francisco Palou founded the Mission Dolores and conducted the first mass in October 1776. There is hardly any mention by these settlers of American Indians. Perhaps the inconvenience of being on an isolated point of land surrounded by salt water led the natives to live elsewhere.

The United States tried in 1835 to buy the entire Bay area from Mexico. Reports of the magnificent, sheltered harbor had reached Washington, and there were many who believed the United States needed a Pacific Ocean port. The Mexican government declined the offer. Meanwhile, the city's first non-Mexican residence was constructed on land we know today as modern San Francisco. The dwelling was humility itself: an English seafarer named

William Richardson put up a tent he made out of part of his ship's sail. The area at the time was called Yerba Buena.

U.S. Navy Captain John B. Montgomery sailed into the bay in 1846, shortly after hostilities began elsewhere between the U.S. and Mexico. He and his well-armed men went ashore and marched into a plaza where they unfurled the American flag. There was no resistance. The city was renamed San Francisco the following year, though calling the site a city was still wishful thinking. There were, in 1846, just 700 whites (half of them American), plus 150 Indians, Hawaiians, and African-Americans. The following year, U.S. citizens outnumbered Mexicans; the area's Americanization had begun.

Prospectors search for gold in a California creek.

Gold!

Gold was discovered outside San Francisco in 1848. Approximately eighty thousand gold prospectors, or '49ers, as they were called, rushed to northern California, believing they could dig gravel in any northern California streambed and get rich. The lure of gold was so strong that sailors abandoned ships in the bay to head inland and explore. When the Civil War began in 1861, hundreds of men left their hometowns, apparently to fight. But some without strong ties veered west instead, hoping to strike it rich. Few did, but fewer still returned home. Some prospered. Levi Strauss, a merchant, made pants from a denim material intended for tents. The dark-blue pants were snapped up by the miners, and a pioneering San Francisco business was born.

San Francisco became a city of twenty thousand tents as people from all over showed up attempting to hit paydirt. And for every miner there was someone willing to take his money. The Bay area was nicknamed The Barbary Coast because of the gamblers, hustlers, swindlers, and prostitutes who took advantage of prospectors. Many ended up broke — or injured or dead — without ever panning any of the streams that ran down the western slopes of the Sierra Nevada mountains. The government was corrupt, too. In one case of blatant bribery, a franchise for streetcars was obtained by a United Railroads executive seen entering City Hall with a shoebox filled with cash.

Early Chinatown, San Francisco.

The Chinese Arrive

The very first Chinese to come to the United States may have been a Cantonese named Chum Ming. He arrived in San Francisco in 1847 and later spread word of the gold rush to his countrymen, who came to San Francisco in 1849 at a rate that soon alarmed many white citizens. San Francisco's Chinese population deserves special attention for several reasons. First, the vast majority arrived to work and save before returning to their families in Asia. They had no intention of becoming Americans. Second, San Francisco today has the largest Chinatown in the United States. And third, San Francisco's Chinese community is fascinating because attitudes toward the Chinese have changed almost completely from the time they first set foot here to today.

By 1880 an estimated seventy-five thousand Chinese had immigrated to the United States. Almost all of them worked for woefully inadequate wages, and most lived in the Bay area. They worked in the gold mines and became a great source of labor on America's first transcontinental railroad, the Union Pacific. Their willingness to perform the lowliest work and their culture, which seemed entirely alien to white Americans, caused them to become detested by some residents. Bret Harte, the writer of western fiction, reported that a mob of boys stoned to death a Chinese man named Wan Lee in the streets of San Francisco in 1869. Harte pointed out that the crowd was made up of "Christian school children."

Had these misguided children realized the difficulty in just reaching California and the dedication it took to make the voyage, they might have held their fire. The average voyage across the Pacific took two months. Young Chinese men paid virtually everything they had in exchange for rotten food, theft, and violence. One crew of Americans lined their passengers up and cut off their braided pigtails. The Chinese retaliated by killing the captain and crew and allowing the ship to run aground in the South Pacific. Another ship, which sailed from Hong Kong in 1854, arrived in San Francisco with one hundred of its five hundred passengers dead.

The Chinese who went looking for gold did not go it alone, as did white prospectors, but cooperatively. They were able to work large sections of gold-bearing streams by helping each other move huge trees and using many hands to sift nuggets of gold from silty gravel. They must have been successful, because in 1850 a Foreign Miner's License, costing twenty dollars per person per month, was enacted. The effect of such fees would be to discourage miners who worked in teams as the Chinese did. And after California Governor John Bigler delivered a speech calling the Chinese dangerous, they were attacked with increasing frequency.

Top: Modern-day Chinatown, San Francisco.
Bottom: Two Chinatown residents.

How things change. After the gold rush, Chinese men (there were a hundred Chinese men for every Chinese woman in the United States at the time) sent for their families and settled into laundry, restaurant, grocery, and other jobs in San Francisco and elsewhere. Working hard and living simply, they saw to it that their children received all of the education that public schooling could provide. Today, while San Francisco does have a Chinatown, many Chinese-Americans no longer speak a Chinese dialect, and they live all over the Bay area and beyond.

Other Ethnic Groups

In addition to the Chinese, several other ethnic groups have made their marks on San Francisco. In their own ways, they are as responsible for providing the city with atmosphere and an identity as are cable cars and the Golden Gate Bridge.

World War II brought African-Americans to San Francisco, increasing what had been a very small minority. Blacks worked during the war in shipyards, where boats were produced for the war in the Pacific. Having come primarily from the U.S. South, these laborers bought houses or rented rooms in San Francisco's Hunter's Point and Fillmore districts, where Japanese-Americans had been removed as a result of the government's irrational notion that Americans of Japanese descent might cooperate with the enemy. Sons and daughters of this wave of Blacks have found better opportunities than in most other major cities and they now account for their share of politicians, judges, educators, clergy, and civil servants.

Executive Order 9066, which was issued in 1942, wiped out San Francisco's Japanese-American community for the entire duration of World War II. Foreign-born and native alike, 110,000 in all, were sent to inland relocation centers, which in reality were concentration camps. Ironically, a unit of Japanese-American soldiers won medals for bravery in Italy during the war. The Japan Town of today is a few modest blocks east of Fillmore Street. A few second-generation Japanese-Americans go there for special occasions, but they, too, have become a widespread and well-integrated part of society. In fact, probably the only crowd consisting exclusively of Japanese are visitors from Japan on tour buses.

The ethnic makeup of San Francisco's Mission district has gone from Spanish to Mexican to miscellaneous and back to a mix of Spanish-speaking people from Mexico and Central America. Mixed in with these groups are small numbers of Samoans and American Indians. Many are engaged in service jobs as they learn English and try to climb the economic ladder.

Filipinos came to the United States following World War II, setting up their modest shops on the edge of Chinatown and in other neighborhoods, or performing service jobs. They represent less than three percent of the population, totaling perhaps twenty-five thousand people. Their sons and daughters have learned English and become part of northern California society.

European ethnics, especially Italians, have helped flavor the city, too. There were forty-one thousand natives of Italy among San Francisco residents as late as

Fisherman's Wharf is popular with tourists.

1970. Several moved into the seafood business, either as fishermen or as restaurant owners. Fisherman's Wharf once was thick with Italians selling fresh crab and other catches from their pushcarts. Today, the wharf is lined with large restaurants, many of them Italian owned. Italians also play important civic, political, and business roles.

The Quake of 1906 and Other Events of Note

San Francisco's history is marked by events and movements that have had a terrific effect on many people's lives. In some cases, people controlled the events; in others, it was the events that controlled people. The infamous San Francisco earthquake and fire took place on April 18-19, 1906, killing 530 residents and causing $350 million in damage. Had the disaster hit nine years later, it might have disrupted the very first transcontinental telephone call, from New York to San Francisco, placed by Alexander Graham Bell to his coworker, Thomas A. Watson. A year later, in 1916, a bomb was detonated during a local pro-war Preparedness Day parade. A labor organizer and a shoe factory worker were convicted of the blast, which killed ten persons. The two were pardoned in 1939.

World War II, Korea, and Vietnam all involved masses of troops shipping westward across the U.S. in order to reach Asia and other places in the east, and San Francisco became a place where soldiers and sailors had a final fling before combat. After the war, because of its generally tolerant nature, San Francisco became (along with New York City's Greenwich Village) a haven for people whose views and lifestyles were offbeat. It was a place where beatniks listened to poetry or progressive jazz music in bars and coffeehouses, lamenting the material world. Beats became the objects of many jokes in the 1950s, but their movement spawned the immensely influential counterculture of the 1960s — and it all began in San Francisco.

The Counterculture

The 1960s counterculture, or hippie movement, was a blend of many ingredients. Innovative West Coast bands were playing in San Francisco, including Jefferson Airplane, The Grateful Dead, and Big Brother and the Holding Company. Simultaneously, post-WW II young-adult baby boomers matured into a bulge in the population—and they were everywhere. The city was picturesque and relaxed, an ideal spot for experiments in communal living. America's obsessions with money and war made teens and young adults feel there were better ways to lead their lives. Just as important, the University of California in nearby Berkeley lived up to its reputation as a longtime haunt of anti-establishment activists and folks who operated on the fringes of society.

The 1989 earthquake left parts of San Francisco in a shambles. The quake lasted only fifteen seconds but killed sixty-two people.

The intersection of Haight and Ashbury streets, the heart of the 1960s counterculture.

Allen Ginsberg

By literary standards, *Howl* is a wonderful poem. By most other standards, the author of the poem is a strange, complex, and interesting person, typical of the kinds of people attracted to the San Francisco Bay area following World War II.

Allen Ginsberg was born in Paterson, New Jersey, in 1926. His father was an English teacher and his mother was an invalid, confined at one time to a mental institution. Both were Jewish. Ginsberg attended Columbia University in New York, discovering many things about himself and the world — drug addiction, left-wing politics, homosexuality, Eastern religion, free-form poetry, a fascination with chaos, and several people who thought as he did.

Ginsberg did not become the leading poet of America's Beat generation overnight. The balding, bearded man traveled widely and worked at all sorts of jobs, from kitchen helper to market researcher. All the while he thought about writing and poetry and connected his poems to those of the late Walt Whitman and to modern, improvisational jazz. His literary influences also included Jack Kerouac and fellow New Jersey poet William Carlos Williams.

Centers of 1950s beatnik culture included New York City's Greenwich Village and San Francisco. Ginsberg frequented the San Francisco area after studying Buddhism in Asia and learning to love everyone, even his enemies. Such a philosophy helped nurture the hippie movement, which bloomed in northern California in the mid-1960s. So did a widely circulated poster showing Ginsberg dressed as Uncle Sam!

The movement, which lasted just four or five years, was centered at the corner of Haight and Ashbury streets in San Francisco. This became hippie heaven and in 1967 was the center of the city's fabled "summer of love." But with notoriety, things all too soon deteriorated. The tour buses stalled traffic, young people suffered from disease and died from drug use, and the movement ran out of energy. But for several years, San Francisco influenced, and was influenced by, everyone from the Beatles to kids all over the world — and their concerned parents. To this day, the city has kept its bohemian reputation, which may help explain its appeal to gay people.

Larger cities on the whole are more tolerant of homosexuality; and yet the Bay area is unusually accepting, perhaps because through the years it has spawned free thinkers, beatniks, and radicals who were outsiders themselves and who tolerated fellow outsiders. Once San Francisco became known as a town with numerous gays, other gay people migrated there, feeling they would be treated equitably and that there would be support systems for their social, personal, and medical needs. While sexual orientation may not have ceased entirely to be an issue in political races or in private-sector hiring, far greater worries, such as HIV and AIDS, have become common concerns of gay and straight people alike in all walks of life. Many homosexuals are politically active, believing that the system should work for them as well as it does for other minorities. There have been gay members elected to the City Council, and former Mayor Diane Feinstein, elected to the U.S. Senate in 1992, courted the gay vote during her successful mayoral and senatorial campaigns.

Who Lives in San Francisco Today?

According to a 1990 survey, San Francisco is about 54 percent European-American, 29 percent Asian-Pacific Islander, 11 percent African-American,

0.5 percent American Indian, Inuit, or Aleut, and less than 6 percent other ethnic groups. About 14 percent of the population consists of Spanish-speaking people of various backgrounds. In all, there are 723,959 San Franciscans and 6,253,311 throughout the Bay area, which includes Oakland and San Jose.

San Francisco can only grow up; it cannot grow out because it covers a peninsula surrounded by water on three sides and other municipalities on the fourth. Equally important, because of the danger of earthquakes, San Franciscans can't build any way they choose. Instead, they must observe rigid rules that make structures as quakeproof as technically and financially possible.

The Appeal of the City by the Bay

The city is remarkably hilly. In fact, there are some blocks where the sidewalk is nothing but steps, and cars are ticketed if they are parked without their tires cocked safely into the curb. Rows of vibrant pastel Victorian houses that command great prices are kept in wonderful repair and are in great demand. Winters are rainy and mild, springs sunny and mild, summers foggy and cool, and falls sunny and warm. The summer fogs are created by warm ocean air meeting cold water that washes in along the Pacific Coast.

The speed limit on the zigzag called Lombard Street is five miles per hour!

Despite the quakes, visitors continue to make tourism the city's biggest business. San Francisco also is a leading seaport, with many residents employed in businesses related directly or indirectly to shipping. Exports, which are sent across the Pacific, include raw materials such as cotton, grain, lumber, machinery, paper, and petroleum products. Similarly, the city is a communications center between North America and the Pacific Rim of nations. Also a leader in banking, insurance, and investment, the city has major industrial pursuits and is heavily involved in all facets of the computer business, from manufacturing hardware to thinking up new software.

San Francisco is large enough and cosmopolitan enough to be plagued by the usual ills of urban life. And yet, many of its qualities — a moderate climate, an intriguing landscape, a culture that has not only historically accepted but made welcome a varied and eccentric populace — have made the city attractive to many types of people and enterprises. These qualities have also paid off for the city itself.

From its architecture to its institutions of higher learning and social service systems, its tourism industry to its position in the international marketplace; from its appeal to big business and manufacturing alike to its cuisine and its pro sports teams and other forms of entertainment — San Francisco has clearly benefited in many ways from its diverse, freewheeling, and accepting urban personality.

Signs and people crowd New Orleans' French Quarter.

CHAPTER SEVEN

New Orleans

ourists in the French Quarter of New Orleans on a recent, hot afternoon could hear music above the din of traffic. Rounding a corner, they saw a traditional New Orleans-style funeral. A Dixieland band led the mourners, dressed in everything from century-old costumes to the latest styles, as a horse-drawn wagon carried the coffin. The visitors followed the rhythmic procession of horns, drums, and tambourines into an ancient, mossy cemetery — where all the graves were above ground! New Orleans is one of the few places on earth where coffins are placed inside concrete tombs on top of the ground. If they were buried, they would quickly wash away.

Calling New Orleans low-lying is like saying crayfish swim. In fact, the city is five feet below sea level, so if you dig down a few feet anywhere, you will hit water. The Mississippi River forms a horseshoe shape as it flows constantly through town, and a huge lake named Pontchartrain sits on the city's northern edge. Between the two is a crescent-shaped urban area from which New Orleans got its nickname: "The Crescent City."

The salty Gulf of Mexico is 110 miles to the east and south. Of the three bodies of water, the Mississippi is the most unpredictable. Down through history, heavy rains or snowmelt in faraway places such as Minnesota or Illinois or Ohio have surged downstream, inundating everything. Fortunately, earlier residents built huge mounds running parallel to the river, called levees, to keep the water within its banks.

New Orleans is getting further from the site where fresh water meets salt water all the time. That's because the sluggish, muddy Mississippi deposits its silty contents where it meets the sea, pushing the mouth farther and farther into the Gulf of Mexico as it drops silt in the shape of a huge, flat fan many miles wide. This fan, which is today called the Mississippi Delta, has formed low-lying, fertile plains for hundreds of thousands of years.

France and the Cajun Connection

What is today the city of New Orleans was founded by in 1718 by the French, whose merchants needed an inland water route to Biloxi, in what is now the state of Mississippi, eastward along the Gulf Coast. New Orleans was named after France's Duke of Orleans. Engineers who began to clear the area with convict labor quickly found out what they were up against. Hurricanes swept through in 1721 and 1722, the swamps were filled with mosquitoes, and the water table was only a few feet below wherever they stood.

From the beginning, New Orleans was a real mix of people. The first settlers included Canadian frontiersmen, French troops, convicts, slaves, prostitutes, and various persons without homes. Of 470 adults counted in a 1721 census, 277 were European, 172 were African slaves, and 21 were American Indian slaves. There were a few persons of Spanish origin, and the local natives were Choctaws. Equally skilled in the use of bow and arrow or blowgun and thus capable of surviving in rough terrain, the Choctaws edged further into bayou country as the French expanded their claim.

French-speaking people came and settled from several directions. During the French and Indian War, when Great Britain took control of Canada's Acadian (Atlantic) provinces, French-Canadian settlers were expelled. Some returned to France, some settled in the Caribbean, and some sailed around the eastern half of what would become the United States to land in New Orleans in 1755. These Acadians would become Louisiana Cajuns (a name derived from *Acadians*), speaking a version of French and having an influence on southern Louisiana culture that endures to the present.

Creole, Caribbean, and Other Flavors

Other long-time residents with modern influence are the Creoles. *Creole* can mean different things in different parts of North and South America. Its special ethnic mix may include Spanish, Portuguese, non-Cajun French, and African-Caribbean. But the key word is *mix*, and Creoles have added a way of looking at life that makes Louisiana and especially New Orleans different from anywhere else in the U.S. Frequently discriminated against, Creoles — like Cajuns — have honed their music, their celebrating, and their cooking abilities to art forms. Creole food, a spicy mix combining seafoods with okra, tomatoes, and other fresh vegetables, is one of the world's great cuisines.

Not all of New Orleans' Black slaves shared the same roots. Some came directly from Africa to the port of New Orleans, while others were born in the French colony of St. Dominique, which today is the nation of Haiti in the Caribbean Sea. The Dominicans brought to Louisiana a unique religion, having mixed French Roman Catholicism with the West African practice of voodoo — a cult that included sorcery, curses, trances, communication with ancestors, even the sacrifice of animals.

Farmers and planters of many European nationalities moved in, growing tobacco, sugar cane, and indigo for dye. The port of New Orleans failed to meet French expectations, in part because the crops grown in the area were bulky but did not produce a lot of cash. Napoleon needed money to pursue his goals in Europe and in 1803 offered what is now much of the central United States for $15 million. Thomas Jefferson persuaded legislators to make the Louisiana Purchase, and millions of acres switched from French to U.S. rule.

The population at that time included 4,000 people of European descent, 2,700 slaves and about 1,300 other "persons of color." Several languages, including English, French, and Spanish, could be heard throughout the city.

A Land of Conflict

In 1804, African slaves successfully rose up against their French masters in the Caribbean. Led by Toussaint L'Ouverture, the slaves declared their independence by starting the Republic of Haiti. Word of this defeat of French troops reached slaves in North America, especially those living in New Orleans and other areas formerly owned by France.

The Battle of New Orleans, 1815.

Slaves in Louisiana's sugar cane country, led by Charles Deslonde, overpowered their masters on January 8, 1811, and met at several prearranged places with fugitives already living in the woods. As many as five hundred slaves, armed with knives and tools, marched toward New Orleans. Terrified whites scattered as the army moved south. On January 10, the rebels were met by a hundred well-armed militiamen and thirty federal troops. What followed wasn't really a battle, since the whites had guns and the slaves did not.

At the time of Deslonde's rebellion, the vast area of the Louisiana Purchase, north and west of New Orleans, was inhabited by but a few frontierspeople and American Indians. Despite its thin population, however, it was bitterly contested during the War of 1812, a war between the U.S. and Britain that ended with the British burning Washington, D.C., and the U.S. victorious in several other battles. But the biggest victory, the Battle of New Orleans, came on January 8, 1815 — two weeks after the signing of the Treaty of Ghent had ended the war. U.S. soldiers under Andrew Jackson slaughtered an invading British army that had not received word of the war's end.

A Crowded Place

New Orleans from 1820 to the Civil War in 1861 was a nice place for most white residents and a haven for many Blacks. The gateway to the country's largest river and a growing international port, the city was a big market for cotton, sugar, and slaves. Runaway slaves found New Orleans large enough to conceal their presence. In fact, the mayor grumbled to the city council in 1830 that the great number of runaways "crowd in the city, hide, and make our city a den." The runaways mixed with free Blacks, who were more numerous in New Orleans than anywhere in the South at the time except Charleston, South Carolina.

German and Irish immigrants arrived in New Orleans in large numbers in the late 1840s, driven out of Europe by revolution, repression, or famine. The city's population by 1850 was 116,375, a figure that taxed public facilities to the point of danger. Drainage was poor, and the city had no sewage system. Consequently, New Orleans drinking water sometimes became tainted, causing outbreaks of cholera and yellow fever. The worst epidemic, yellow fever in 1853, resulted in the deaths of more than eight thousand residents.

The Hardships of Civil War and More Growing Pains

New Orleans and Louisiana joined other Southern states in seceding from the Union in 1861, which helped ignite the Civil War. Union forces captured New Orleans in the spring of 1862, bringing imports and exports to a halt. Union General Benjamin F. Butler, an early champion of equal rights for African-American and other working people, ran the city. He ordered the execution of a resident caught tearing down the U.S. flag and he seized Confederate property. Though Butler improved sanitary conditions, the crotchety general managed to insult diplomats at several foreign consuls and was recalled before the war ended. Fortunately, the city's romantic Vieux Carre (its "Old Town" or French Quarter) was untouched by the conflict.

New Orleans did not fully recover from the war until about 1880. Yet by the beginning of the twentieth century, things were booming. The population totaled 187,104 in 1900 and would have been larger but for the fact that lack of drainage slowed development. A screw-type electric pump installed in 1917 greatly improved drainage, so that by the 1930s low-lying areas were as dry as higher sites. With the levee holding back the river and the port modernized, New Orleans was on the move.

Water was both enemy and friend to residents. Lots of money was spent to wipe out mosquitoes and to quarantine unhealthy goods that constantly arrived by ship from abroad. On the other hand, shipping helped New Orleans weather the Great Depression of the 1930s better than many other cities; by the end of World War II, it had become the second-largest U.S. port.

Improvements and Integration

The two decades following World War II saw many construction projects and the skillful preservation of many of the city's oldest public and private buildings. It also saw the demand by African-Americans, who represented about 45 percent of the 1960 population of 630,000, for equality. One of the reasons the integration of schools took place peaceably in New Orleans was that church leaders of all races urged their flocks not to interfere with progress. But despite the harmonious message, many white children were removed from public schools and enrolled in parochial or private institutions.

The annual Mardi Gras parade draws thousands of visitors.

Mardi Gras, a thoroughly New Orleans tradition that borrows its reason for being from Catholicism, is one of the world's great festivals. *Mardi Gras*, which means "Fat Tuesday," is the day before Lent begins, forty weekdays prior to Easter. Lent is a time of penitence, of giving up favored things in respect for the sacrifice of Jesus on the cross. In contrast, Mardi Gras revelers give up nothing. The party season actually begins with the new year. More than sixty organizations hold formal, private balls, and many hold parades. The parades, which start about two weeks before Mardi Gras, feature large and expensive floats. The fun ends at midnight on Mardi Gras night, when Lent begins.

The "Other" Music of New Orleans

Everyone knows Dixieland and jazz trace their roots to New Orleans. But not many know that rock 'n' roll was influenced by tunes that originated among Black laborers working under the hot Mississippi Delta sun.

New Orleans' version of rock 'n' roll was first heard by outsiders following World War II. David and Julian Braund, owners of a small New Jersey recording company, heard New Orleans-style rhythm and blues and made money recording Roy Brown's "Good Rockin' Tonight" and other tunes prior to 1950. Imperial Records then signed Antoine ("Fats") Domino in 1949, and he cranked out several hits, from "Blueberry Hill" to "I'm Walkin'" to "My Blue Heaven." These million-sellers brought the city and its talent international recognition.

Various record companies jumped on the Louisiana bandwagon and signed a host of musicians with New Orleans roots: Ray Charles, Professor Longhair, Lloyd Price, Guitar Slim, Little Richard, Clarence Henry, Smiley Lewis, and more. Their songs influenced everyone from Elvis Presley to the Beatles and the Rolling Stones.

Most of the musicians and vocalists were African-Americans, though neither Black nor white talent made much money from recording. Yet such talented local producers as Harold Battiste and Allen Toussaint continued to record whoever showed promise. Strong vocals mixed with strong drums, a heavy bass, and light piano and horns to enliven everything from Girl Scout sock hops to college fraternity parties.

Despite falling out of favor in the 1960s, the New Orleans sound is strong today. With its invigorating blend of French-Cajun dance tunes, Caribbean rhythms, and African-American blues, one brand of Louisiana music — zydeco — has taken other cities in North America by storm. And one group of New Orleans musicians who continue to make an impact are the Neville Brothers. Their sweet-voiced songs, influenced by classic rhythm and blues, soul, reggae, and more, are international hits, though the four perform only occasionally outside the Crescent City.

Who Lives in New Orleans?

According to one 1990 survey, modern New Orleans has a city population of 496,938 and a metropolitan area containing 1,238,816 residents. It is nearly 62 percent Black, 35 percent white, 2 percent Asian-Pacific Islander, and less than 1 percent American Indian. About 3.5 percent of the population consists of Spanish-speaking people of various ethnic groups. This relatively simple-sounding mix of mainly white and Black belies the fact that many who trace their ancestors into the Louisiana past find a gumbo of race, ethnicity, and language.

Dixieland jazz can be heard all over New Orleans.

Modernity presses relentlessly at New Orleans. Although it continues to be among America's most attractive and exotic cities, both the city and its people feel the pressure to conform. On St. Charles Avenue, the picturesque streetcar must compete with multiple lanes of much faster automobile traffic. A portion of the magnificent old southern homes on the street are preserved, but many have been replaced by apartments, condominiums, and offices. Palmetto and magnolia trees remain, but they shade fewer and fewer horse-drawn wagons or sweet-voiced Black women selling berries. Like all cities, New Orleans continues to change. But perhaps more so than others, it also finds much in its past that is well worth preserving.

Art Deco hotels gleam against the blue sky of Miami Beach.

CHAPTER EIGHT

Miami

Centuries before there was a city of Miami, there was a land called Florida. Hundreds of years before there was a Florida, a group of American Indians known as the Tequesta lived in a village on what is now Miami's Biscayne Bay, which is part of the Atlantic Ocean. Those first people were tall, barely clothed in deerhide, and sometimes tattooed. The Tequesta hunted, fished, and grew corn, beans, and squash. They also foraged, gathering edible plants, fruits, berries, seeds, and roots.

Florida before Europeans arrived was thinly settled. A tribe or clan of American Indians could walk for days along the beach, through sharp-edged fields of sawgrass or into low, thick swamps without seeing another human. Indians had the area so much to themselves that they sometimes traded with others by rowing their dugout boats as far as the island of Cuba, ninety miles to the southeast. Such isolation changed early in the sixteenth century with the landing of Spanish explorers.

The Tequesta, together with the Calusa, Timucua, and other American Indians, were captured by the Spanish troops and used as slaves and servants. Many died of beatings or of diseases borne by the European soldiers. The peninsula of Florida was claimed at different times by Spain, England, and the U.S., but by the early 1700s it was almost devoid of American Indians.

Into this subtropical land came the Seminole. They were made up primarily of battle-weary Creek Indians, but they also included in their number many runaway African-American slaves. The group was fleeing the colonization of what is now the state of Georgia, and even their name — *Seminole* — is a Creek word for "runaway" that may have come from *cimarrón*, a Spanish word for a domesticated animal that has returned to the wild. Fearless Seminole leaders such as Coacoochee, Micancopy, and Osceola kept their people free in the 1800s, though U.S. troops used trickery to capture the leaders and their warriors.

A few stubborn Seminoles resisted attempts to send them to reservations far to the west in Oklahoma. Instead, they moved deeper into southern Florida's vast Everglades marshlands (which today mark Miami's western

Alligator wrestling remains a popular tourist attraction.

limits), where they were all but forgotten by newcomers. Resistance to government domination became a way of life for the Seminole, and technically, they have never made peace by signing a treaty with the United States. Only a few thousand remain in southern Florida today.

The U.S. acquired Florida from Spain in 1819 and soon built Fort Dallas, where present-day Miami stands. The fort was constructed to house troops in search of Seminoles who had been unwilling to move west. Down through the nineteenth century, a few permanent residents arrived, among them former slaves after the Civil War. Although Florida seceded with the rest of the South in 1861, slavery before the war — and resentment afterward — was less intense than in Georgia, South Carolina, and elsewhere. Consequently, some freed slaves actually moved further south to be in Florida.

"The Mother of Miami"

Not even the most optimistic Floridian would have called Miami a city when Julia Tuttle, "the mother of Miami," settled there in 1891. The first home, in what is now Coconut Grove, was built that same year, while the first church, the Roman Catholic Holy Name, was erected in 1896. A post office had existed at the ruined Fort Dallas since 1850, but except for a couple of plantations and a trading post, there was nothing else.

Tuttle was a widow who had visited the area earlier from Cleveland with Frederick, her husband. They were wealthy, and because Frederick had tuberculosis, they were in search of good weather year-round. At the time, the best way to reach Miami was to sail by steamboat from New York City to Key West, then catch a mail boat and head briefly northward. The only other way to reach Miami was to sail to Daytona Beach and then walk south for 250 miles along the beach with the mail carrier!

Tuttle had a better idea. The winter of 1895 included a hard freeze that destroyed Florida's citrus crop, which at the time was grown in northern and

Hotels along Miami Beach in 1924.

central parts of the state. Tuttle sent railroad baron Henry Flagler a bunch of orange blossoms untouched by frost, pointing out that frosts were unknown so far south. The next year, Flagler extended his railroad from Indian River to Miami. As oranges chugged north to consumers, tourists chugged south to sunshine and sandy beaches — and Julia Tuttle became the only woman to found a major U.S. city.

The Building Boom Begins

The Florida East Coast Railway soon brought African-American and white laborers to build the city being developed by Tuttle's Biscayne Bay

Company. The men lived in tents along the shore while they constructed her first project, the Miami Hotel. The wooden structure began as a bunkhouse and was razed by fire in 1899, but the area must have impressed people, for by 1900 sixteen hundred permanent residents were living in Miami.

Early settlers included soldiers quartered there during the Spanish-American War, which was fought in Cuba and elsewhere in 1898. Others drifted in, including Spanish-speaking people from Puerto Rico, Cuba, and smaller Caribbean islands. They found work building and managing estates for wealthy northerners. One such early mansion, Villa Vizcaya, still stands and is open to the public. Seminoles poled their dugouts cautiously into the growing city to trade otter skins, buckskins, alligator hides, and bird plumes. Clad in turbans and long shirts, they probably were the first American Indians ever seen by well-to-do visitors from New York, Philadelphia, and Boston.

Villa Vizcaya.

Julia Tuttle was not the only person in Miami to make a living from real estate. The city, with six thousand residents by 1911, soon became a fashionable place. Developers pushed back the underbrush to offer seaside building lots. Millionaire businessman Carl Fisher financed the dredging of Biscayne Bay in 1915, creating the strip of sand parallel to the shoreline that

Osceola, patriot and warrior

Osceola had reasons to dislike white people. Shortly after his birth in 1804, his father died in a battle between whites and Indians. The boy and his mother fled south from Georgia to Florida, pursued by Tennessee raiders and troops under General Andrew Jackson. The two were released after promising to peacefully return to Georgia.

Instead, they drifted south to join the Seminole, a tribe made up of various American Indians plus runaway slaves and persons of mixed race.

The young warrior had two wives and several children. One day, slavehunters pounced on Osceola's first wife and took her to Georgia, claiming that one of her ancestors was an African slave. Osceola was further incensed when, as a chief, he was told that the U.S. would not recognize him and fellow chiefs as leaders unless they signed a treaty with the government. He drew his knife, proclaimed, "This is the way I will sign all such treaties," and plunged the blade through the paper.

Osceola backed his words with deeds. He killed a Seminole chief who had signed the treaty, thereby volunteering to move his people to Oklahoma. Osceola also ambushed a party of soldiers. This attack was one cause of the Seminole War, which began in 1835 and lasted until 1842. Osceola fought until 1837, when he agreed to hold peace talks with white officers, in part because he had little energy from his struggle with chronic malaria. Outnumbered and surrounded by heavily armed U.S. soldiers, the Seminoles were quickly captured, and Osceola was sent to prison in Fort Moultrie, South Carolina. Though he appears healthy in a painting done in prison, the thirty-four-year-old leader died of a throat infection a few days after the painting was finished. Although he died a prisoner, Osceola secured a place in history by giving the ancestors of today's Seminoles the courage to remain in Florida.

is today's Miami Beach. After World War I, President Warren G. Harding came south to winter in Miami, and middle-class Americans from all over moved to or vacationed in this subtropical area.

The City's Growing Pains

African-Americans, Latinos, and most other Miami residents were hurt less by a 1925 real-estate slump than by a hurricane that swamped the city in 1926. Housing had been hastily and poorly constructed, particularly for persons working as laborers, field hands, hotel maids, and garment makers. And partly because people living in Miami's warm climate did not need a lot of money to stay alive, employers felt justified in paying out low wages. Prohibition, the national ban on alcoholic beverages, created illegal work as a stream of boats retrieved rum and other liquor from Cuba and elsewhere in the Caribbean and turned Miami into a port city for the illicit distribution of alcohol.

The population grew relentlessly in the 1920s, from thirty thousand to one hundred thousand in five years. This population explosion caused Police Chief H. Leslie Quigg to search for patrolmen so far beyond Miami that he recruited white plowhands living in Georgia. The poorly trained officers frightened many of the city's three hundred thousand annual winter visitors at the time, as well as the locals. In one incident, a policeman shot at a jaywalker! He missed his target but hit another pedestrian a block away.

Some patrolmen probably were members of the Ku Klux Klan, the racist terrorist group that reached peak membership and visibility in the 1920s. Its white-supremacist, anti-Semitic members were recruited openly and met in the light of burning crosses on the beach. Meanwhile, the city's hotel industry began attracting Blacks from outside Miami, including several hundred from the Bahamas who became residents of the Coconut Grove neighborhood. While the Klan has expanded and declined in Florida over the years, the link between Coconut Grove and the Bahamas continues to be strong. Bahamian-style wooden homes still stand on Charles Street, and Miami's Goombay festival has become one of the largest Black heritage festivals in the U.S.

The Ku Klux Klan met openly in Miami's early days.

A City of Diversity

Miami had Seminoles to thank in the '30s for two very different attractions. One huge tourist attraction — alligator wrestling — had, ironically, been taught to the Seminoles by a white Florida farmboy, Henry Coppinger, Jr. The other attraction, also taken from Seminole life, was the Orange Bowl parade, originally the Palm Festival, a local native American parade and party. The first Orange Bowl parade took place in 1934.

Miami's weather, which averages about seventy-five degrees each year, has attracted the famous and the infamous alike. At a 1933 Miami news conference, President Franklin D. Roosevelt watched as a bullet from a deranged gunman whizzed past him and killed Chicago Mayor Anton Cermak. At about the same time, Chicago mobster Al Capone began spending his winters in Miami. Local people with national fame included Katherine Rawls, a record-breaking swimmer and diver throughout the 1930s, and Joseph Widener, who in 1931 pushed through legalized gambling and built Hialeah, which remains today one of the nation's top horse-racing tracks.

World War II soldiers, sailors, and airmen passed through Miami, no doubt dazzled by the city's string of small, snazzy art deco hotels and by the glorious seafront, set against Miami's perpetually deep-blue sky. Jewish and other residents from New York, New Jersey, and elsewhere along the seaboard continued to retire in the area. Today, 17 percent of the population is over the age of sixty-five, almost twice as high a percentage as that of retirees living in Phoenix, Arizona, a Southwest retirement destination.

Following World War II, the area was hit by another wave of growth, during which additional Puerto Ricans and other Caribbean residents came and prospered. But prosperity only brushed the area's African-Americans. Making up about 15 percent of Miami's 1950 population of 249,276, Blacks seldom found work except in South Florida's huge new juice-concentrate business, in agriculture and food processing, or as cooks, maids, porters, or bellhops in large hotels. Miami's airports handled more than one million passengers a year by 1947, but most travel-related jobs paid badly. Life for Blacks was difficult. As late as the 1950s, there was only one hospital with but thirty beds for African-Americans in all of this segregated city.

In addition to suffering discrimination in housing, employment, and health care, Blacks — along with Jews — became targets of people motivated by racial hatred. On September 22, 1951, a dynamite blast shook Carver Village, where apartments had just been opened to African-American residents. That same year, sticks of dynamite were tossed at The Hebrew School and at the Coral Gables Jewish Center. As destructive and disturbing as the bombings were, they also prompted citizens of various racial and ethnic backgrounds to form the Dade Council of Community Relations. This group was given credit for the peaceful desegregation of public schools in 1961.

A New Influx — Cuban-Americans

The city was becoming more unmanageable at about the time residents voted in 1957 for one government to run Miami and all of Dade County. In 1959, several hundred Cuban refugees, fleeing Fidel Castro's takeover of their island ninety miles away, arrived in Miami. The stream of immigrants continued so that, by 1976, four hundred thousand Miami-area residents were of Cuban origin. Most were disillusioned with Castro's promises, in part broken because the U.S. supported the regime of fallen dictator Fulgencio Batista and opposed Castro's socialist politics.

Cuban-Americans would exceed half a million persons after 1980, when Cuba allowed anyone to leave from the small port of Mariel. Some of these

Calle Ocho (Eighth Street) is Main Street to Miami's Cuban-Americans.

120,000 "Marielito" refugees were criminals and drug addicts, adding to Dade County's law-enforcement woes. Castro allowed this exodus after the United States refused to return Cubans who had skyjacked Fidel's planes, despite Castro's turning over American skyjackers to U.S. authorities.

Marielitos initially were housed beneath freeway overpasses and on the Orange Bowl football field. Today, some are imprisoned, but many more are employed. They have homes and participate in city life. Many speak English as well as their native Spanish. In contrast, Haitians fleeing a military coup on their island find themselves misunderstood or unwelcome because they speak only French and have arrived with few possessions. Many washed up in decrepit boats after 1990, when a cruel dictatorship swept aside Haiti's democratic government. Haitian refugees were returned by the United States to their native island, a move some see as racially motivated.

Blacks and people of Caribbean heritage who have witnessed the social and economic success of many Cubans wonder if race has also played a part in that success. Many Cubans are fair skinned, in contrast to some Puerto Ricans and numerous Haitians and African-Americans. While this distinction may well have favored newly arrived Cubans, other racial factors were at work as well, and not all of them favored the Cuban refugees. Many refugees were greatly resented by English-speaking whites in Miami when Cubans first began living in neighborhoods where Spanish became the primary language.

As to the charges that white racism favored the fair-skinned Cubans, other factors were at work on that score as well. The first Cubans to leave Cuba when Batista fell from power consisted mostly of the upper classes who had money and educations. Some were able to smuggle out their valuables when they left Cuba for Miami. This, combined with any business and family connections they might have already had in Miami, helped them prosper fairly quickly. The lives of these Cubans were thus different than those of poverty-stricken African-American and Caribbean people who came under harsher conditions and had little money or other resources to draw upon.

In some ways, the situation with Miami's early Cuban immigrants resembles that of other immigrant groups, such as Koreans, Arabs, or, in earlier years, Jews, who buy small businesses in poor neighborhoods. Many of these immigrants left their native land as pilots, engineers, or other educated professionals and brought money with them. Despite whatever credit the newcomers deserve for adding to the vitality of their new neighborhoods, their success is certainly little cause for celebration among other minorities.

In Miami, such resentment contributed to the vicious rioting in such inner-city areas as Overtown and Liberty City, which erupted in flames and gunfire following the 1980 beating death of an African-American businessman, killed by white police. Blacks to this day feel discrimination by police, whether the officers are male or female, or of Anglo or Hispanic descent.

With Prosperity Comes Complexity

Miami has a free-trade zone, which is an area where international business can take place without the burden of any country's taxes. It has become the place where businesses from Europe, North America, and South America all meet. Unfortunately, the drug trade has also for years used the same crossroads. Cocaine processed in Colombia comes through Miami's port and airport. So does marijuana from Jamaica. And with the illegal substances come desperate people willing to gamble with their lives for the chance to earn thousands of dollars. Miami's drug culture has contributed to frequent shootings, a sky-high murder rate, and huge sales of guns to criminals and fearful citizens alike.

Yet the city prospers. A boom in the mid-1980s has given the city many new and colorful buildings. There is no better public transportation anywhere than the one-billion-dollar Metrorail, completed in 1984. Nightlife includes Latin and reggae music by dynamic bands. The city's restaurants offer America's freshest seafood and citrus. There is an opera, a symphony for musicians aged twenty-one to thirty, and twenty Spanish-language theaters featuring comedy, puppetry, vaudeville, and satire.

The name *Miami*, which comes from an American Indian term for "big water" or "wide water," seems aptly suited to the city, its people, its positives, and its negatives. Sandwiched between the ocean and the Everglades and resting only a dozen feet above sea level, Miami's 358,548 residents and 1,937,094 metropolitan Dade County residents entertain more than eight million visitors a year. The city is about 66 percent white, 27 percent Black, and 62.5 percent of Hispanic descent from any ethnic group. Less than 1 percent of the population is made up of American Indians and people of Asian-Pacific Island descent, and about 6 percent other ethnic groupings.

Unwelcome visitors vary, from mosquitoes to unpredictable hurricanes that can rock the area in summer and fall. But despite the area's natural and manmade misfortunes — or possibly in part *because* of the area's many problems — some experts see the one-hundred-year-old city truly as a place of the future. Why is that?

First, Miami really is a crossroads among people from North America, South America, the Caribbean, and Europe. Second, it represents the blend of people found in most globally important cities. Third, Miami has intense drug and crime problems and has yet to achieve law-enforcement breakthroughs. Fourth, it caters to those on the top rung of society's ladder and makes room for those on the bottom, while the vast middle takes its work ethic and willingness to pay taxes to the suburbs. And fifth and most important, Miami, for better or worse, is committed to continued growth. Perhaps that is the future, after all.

The pleasing colors and designs of Art Deco can be found all over Miami.

A courtyard in the Spanish governor's mansion, San Antonio.

CHAPTER NINE

San Antonio

Discrimination against African-Americans has greatly overshadowed discrimination against Hispanics in America's past. But as late as the 1950s, signs in some Texas storefronts read, "No dogs or Mexicans allowed." From Hollywood to the government, stereotypes abound of Hispanic-Americans as lazy, immoral people who steal jobs from "Americans." Mexican-Americans find bitter irony in these prejudices because they and their ancestors have had to work at least as hard as Anglos to prosper. They know, too, that the family unit is as strong today among Mexican-Americans as it is among other citizens. All this should be kept in mind when visiting San Antonio.

San Antonio's first European visitors were Spaniards. They established a military post and several religious missions on the site of what had been a Coahuiltecan Indian settlement in 1718. Situated in scrubby, dry, often boiling-hot south-central Texas, the outpost became a source of fresh water and a travelers' rest between Spain's established towns in Mexico and the early French trading posts eastward in Louisiana. The area's first actual non-native settlers came from an unusual location — the Canary Islands in the Atlantic . These people arrived in 1731. They, too, were of Spanish origin, and they drew up plans for a town on the west bank of the San Antonio River.

The sixteen families of Canary Islanders, fifty-six people in all, built huts initially west of the fort, but then shifted to a site closer to the river and fresh water. Plaza of Islanders, which today is San Antonio's Main Street, began to grow. It wasn't easy, however, since the only way to make a living was to raise cattle, and the missionaries had already staked out all the nearby land. Several of the men got jobs as soldiers, taking up weapons to keep the Comanche and other Indians at a distance.

Fear of the Comanche

The Comanche were among the best fighters anywhere. In fact, they were so fierce that Apaches in the vicinity of San Antonio in 1749 made peace with the Spaniards in exchange for the protection of Spanish guns. A French visitor to the "several miserable villages" that made up San Antonio in 1768

Zebulon M. Pike.

found Indian residents to be friendly and generous with whatever they had, while the Spanish acted aloof.

U.S. explorer Zebulon Pike, who passed through San Antonio in 1807, was far more favorably impressed by the site. There were about two thousand residents who seemed to have surplus food and drink for frequent celebrations. In 1811, the revolution that had been cooking against Spain in other parts of Mexico reached San Antonio. Juan Casas, an army officer, tried to recruit the locals but was captured, sent to Mexico in irons by the Spanish, and killed. His head was returned and placed on a pole as a warning to other would-be revolutionaries. Nevertheless, a hastily assembled bunch of Americans, Indians, and Mexicans won a battle with the Spanish military near San Antonio in 1813, only to be ambushed and overwhelmed a few months later by four thousand Spanish troops.

These Spaniards, under General Joaquin de Arredondo, nearly wiped San Antonio off the map. After the battle, the soldiers imprisoned three hundred local men in a granary that was so small, eighteen of the prisoners suffocated. Arredondo imprisoned the women, too, forcing them to serve his soldiers. To make bad matters worse, a drought, a flood, and an epidemic had swept San Antonio, and few free people were around to react to these horrific events.

Americans Invade Texas

By 1820, other momentous things were happening: Americans were given permission to settle in Texas, and a year later, in 1821, Mexico, which included Texas and much of what is now the U.S. Southwest, declared its independence from Spain.

The period between 1820 and the Battle of the Alamo in 1836 saw Americans moving into Texas like tumbleweeds moving across a plain. These people, few of whom spoke Spanish, seemed brash, opportunistic, and disrespectful of the newly free Mexicans. They were well armed and quick to anger, and they failed to act like guests in the huge, empty area that was Texas. They offended General Antonio López de Santa Anna, who was as quick tempered as the new settlers. Santa Anna sent his brother-in-law to San Antonio to stop a movement for an independent Texas, and the brother-in-law fought several battles with Americans around San Antonio. Santa Anna arrived in 1836 and wiped out resistance at the Alamo. What the doomed defenders could not know, however, was that their resistance gave Texans elsewhere time to declare their independence.

Antonio López de Santa Anna.

In 1846 U.S. President James K. Polk ordered General Zachary Taylor to seize disputed Texas land that had been settled by Mexicans. After a border clash, the two sides declared war. Some twelve thousand U.S. troops advanced on the Mexican city of Veracruz and then on to Mexico City in 1847. The following year, Mexico handed over to the U.S. today's Texas, California, Arizona, New Mexico, Nevada, Utah, and part of Colorado. Mexico received $18 million from the U.S. for its lost land.

War Takes Its Toll

San Antonio was slow to recover from warfare with Mexico. Even after Texas became a state in 1845, the area was desolate. As late as 1866, after the U.S. Civil War had ended, the city was plagued by rats. A cholera epidemic at the time killed several hundred people. Only later did citizens take steps to dispose of sewage and garbage in ways that would prevent further health problems, and eventually the region prospered. The Army, with a major headquartered in San Antonio, kept Indians away from white ranchers and farmers, who began great cattle drives near San Antonio, moving their stock from Texas to Kansas for shipment back East.

The drives ended in 1877, the year the first train reached San Antonio. Now ranchers could drive cattle into town, corral them, and wait for them to be loaded into boxcars. Besides cattle for the consumption of beef, sheep were raised for their meat and for wool. Except for the city itself and the ranches near it, all of this part of Texas was open range; the only private land anywhere surrounded precious sources of water. Money realized from the sale of cattle and sheep brought wonderful goods westward on the train to San Antonio. It's no exaggeration to state that once the two thin, parallel tracks of steel showed up, the city boomed.

A new water works tapped the river in 1880 so that fresh water could be piped to everyone. Ambitious construction projects began, and the town became large enough to support streetcars, which were pulled by mules.

The Alamo as it appears today.

What happened at the Alamo?

Following its independence from Spain in 1821, Mexico invited Americans to settle in Texas because Mexico wanted to develop the vast, empty land. Soon American cotton farmers and their slaves outnumbered Mexican settlers. Led by Stephen Austin, Texans asked Mexico if they could apply for U.S. statehood. This upset Mexico because the Americans had originally promised to become Roman Catholic, renounce slavery, and become Mexican citizens. When Austin stirred things up among English-speaking Texans, he was arrested.

President Santa Anna of Mexico believed he could solve things by introducing a constitution that would cover all of his country, including Texas. When Texans (including some of Mexican origin) broke away from Mexico, Santa Anna led six thousand troops into Texas in 1836 to end the rebellion. He and 3,000 troops faced 187 Americans, who had taken refuge in the old San Antonio mission. Colonel William B. Travis and his Alamo defenders, including frontiersman Davey Crockett and slave smuggler James Bowie, lasted ten days. Mexican artillery finally blew down a wall and the attackers poured in. Three Americans survived — a slave owned by Travis named Joe and a woman and her baby. They were spared so they would warn others that Mexico was serious about keeping Texas.

The Texas Army also was defeated by Santa Anna's forces in a town named Goliad before Texans and Mexicans squared off for the third time in 1836. This decisive battle took place in San Jacinto, where the Mexicans were caught by surprise and overwhelmed by American forces. Texas became a republic under Sam Houston before applying for statehood. Though this fight for independence was important, it was eventually overshadowed by the U.S. Civil War — which had been influenced by Texas, a state where slaveowning was permitted.

Pavement replaced the dust that lay in most streets, and the U.S. Army established a permanent fort, called Post Santonio but later named Fort Sam Houston. By 1881, gaslights flickered in the homes of the middle class. At about the same time, a second rail line reached San Antonio, and in 1882 the first telephone exchange was installed. The local electric company began furnishing power for newfangled bulbs in 1887.

The railroad brought in a wave of European immigrants, many of them German. Though the terrain was entirely different from the country of their birth, these people fanned out across southwestern Texas and today are among its leading citizens. Smaller numbers of Germans had arrived immediately after statehood, building tidy, single-story houses of limestone block. First-generation Irish put up small cottages of chalkstone, each with a wide fireplace and huge window shutters. Like people already in the area, the early families prospered. Today, many residents with names such as Gomez or Gutierrez can point to non-Spanish-speaking Europeans in their family trees.

San Antonio in the 1890s

As the nineteenth century neared its end, San Antonio must have been a wonderful place. It featured all of the most modern municipal facilities, yet it retained a blend of Mexican culture and the Wild West. Skilled craftspeople had replaced adobe with Spanish-accented brick buildings surrounded by shady trees and displaying ornate, ornamental iron and tiled roofs. Gardens supported flowers that nodded in the breeze most of the year, plus a central market where all sorts of foods and household goods were available. One of the world's great cuisines, Tex-Mex food, got its start in this part of Texas. Voracious eaters of beef accented their food with Mexican peppers and spices to produce meals that were as addictive as they were fiery.

Despite the rich mix of cultures that flavors San Antonio and other parts of the Southwest, the U.S. government has for decades sent mixed signals about whether people of Mexican origin are welcome in the United States. In 1917, with World War I on, Congress issued special regulations for "temporary workers" from Mexico. Most came, worked, and, feeling no pressure to return, stayed on and became Americans. In contrast, after the Great Depression hit in 1929, as many as half a million Mexican laborers were rounded up and deported. This was especially sad because many of these otherwise law-abiding people were not given normal legal courtesies. Many adults were hustled to the border without their families ever being notified.

The Old Mexico Market House in San Antonio.

Today's San Antonio

The center of modern San Antonio is the San Antonio River. The river was penned up in the 1930s, with flood gates installed to stabilize the river by keeping it from rising or falling too much. A three-mile stretch of the San Antonio, which is horseshoe-shaped, has become a linear park, with recreational, cultural and retail spaces on both sides of the decorative stream. The river isn't wide — it's a snap to toss a stone across it — but it's especially scenic, with many footbridges and thick nests of flowers and shady trees.

The riverwalk, known as Paseo del Rio, includes a Mexican market plaza, where every conceivable craft, snack, food, and kind of music is on display. Shops offer leather goods, dolls, clothing, jewelry, and fiery chili peppers for making authentic Mexican meals at home. Nearby is a 343-acre park, a kiddy park, and the San Antonio Zoo. For persons who have never been to Mexico but want to know what it can be like, this is the place.

Like all large cities, San Antonio has many neighborhoods. Nearest the Alamo is La Villita, now filled with artists of many backgrounds but once a place where everyone spoke Spanish. Bexar, with Main and Military plazas, is the site of the historic Spanish governor's palace. This is where San Antonio's first dwellings were constructed, too.

Another neighborhood is German Town, built originally along a ditch that led from the Alamo. It features homes with architecture not often found in other parts of the Southwest. Mexican Town is much like the rest of the city. Perhaps its best example of the city's roots is the downtown market mentioned earlier, a permanent site for what had been a makeshift vending area for farmers.

According to one 1990 survey, San Antonio's citizen count these days adds up to 935,933, with a metropolitan area containing 1,302,099 Texans. About 72 percent of the population is European-American, 7 percent is African-American, about 1 percent is Asian-Pacific Islander, and less than 1 percent is listed as American Indian. Given San Antonio's historic mix of cultures and peoples, however, perhaps of most interest are two other statistics: 19 percent of various other ethnic groupings, and over 55 percent of Spanish origins from any ethnic group.

The entrance to *El Mercado,* the Old Spanish Market on Dolorosa Street.

Fiesta San Antonio

The city's most popular annual event is Fiesta San Antonio, held in April. It would be a mistake to conclude that the celebration is for tourists. Rather, it pays tribute to the Battle of San Jacinto, when Texas won independence from Mexico, in 1836. The Fiesta features parties, parades with floats, and the selection of a king and a queen.

Steeped in the kind of frontier and cowboy history Americans love, San Antonio is fighting a battle to preserve examples of its past. Many historic sites are deteriorating because of weather and neglect, but a bigger threat has been urban development. For more than sixty years, the Conservation Society (originally made up entirely of San Antonio women) has recommended and succeeded in saving a number of historically important structures. Such dedication is an indication of the fondness so many San Antonians feel about their American city with its Mexican accent.

CHAPTER TEN

Cities and the Future

So much for the past and the present of U.S. cities and the representative sampling featured in the preceding chapters; what will happen in the future? Every American city of any size shares a number of strengths and weaknesses. Among them:

• Too many American cities resemble donuts: the most appealing part is in a ring around a hole in the middle. The ring is the circle of suburbs that attract the businesses, homeowners, and recreational and cultural activities that make metropolitan areas nice places to live. Some cities have become holes into which money is poured to curb crime, stop drug use, keep families together, improve health, retrain persons without skills, and care for young, elderly, and disabled persons. In some metropolitan areas, the suburbs share the financial and social responsibility of keeping alive the cities and the services they provide. In many places, they do not. One way of correcting the imbalance between city and suburbs is to create a single government for both. This is practiced in places such as Indianapolis and Miami, though Miami's crime and drug problems show that one government is no cure-all.

• If suburbs pose a problem to cities, neighborhoods present an opportunity. Chinatowns and Greektowns and Little Italys lure suburban residents and tourists who long for authentic food, music, crafts, and exposure to the kinds of cultures unavailable elsewhere. Cities with distinct neighborhoods, such as Chicago, offer residents and visitors cosmopolitan atmospheres and experiences. On the other hand, some persons who work to maintain distinct neighborhoods really have a hidden motive: to prevent African-Americans, Hispanic-Americans, and other minorities from moving and living where they please. At their best, neighborhoods are a wonderful experience. At their worst, they are islands of bigotry.

• Some cities have put too many eggs in one basket. In other words, they are too dependent on one or two or just a few key industries. Such an example is Detroit, which has always lived or died alongside the health of the U.S. automobile industry. Another, less severe example is Los Angeles, with its emphasis on manufacturing for aerospace and defense. In contrast, cities with

many different kinds of businesses and industries seldom suffer in
all economic areas at once, even
in a nationwide recession. Such
cities would include Chicago,
and, more recently, Seattle,
where airplane manufacturing
has become less crucial because
of the increasing importance of
the city's busy seaport.

• Helping cities out of their
troubles has become a partisan
political issue. A 1992 magazine
ran the following headline: "Bush
to Cities: Drop Dead." This
headline recalled a banner in one
New York tabloid in the 1970s
when President Gerald Ford refused to help bail New York City
out of a financial crisis: "Ford to
NY: Drop Dead." Clearly, some
magazine and newspaper editors
believe Republicans, or at least
George Bush and Gerald Ford,
aren't interested in improving or
restoring America's largest population centers. There may be
some truth in these headlines,
since more Republican voters live
in suburban areas and more

Top: Two young immigrants explore their new American city.
Bottom: A group of young city-dwellers.

Democrats tend to be big-city dwellers. And while the headlines do remind
us that not all Americans share a concern over the health of the nation's cities,
no one honestly believes that walking away from city problems will in any way
improve the country.

• For all their faults, cities remain the most active and most convenient
place to exchange ideas. Rural areas do not have the facilities for trade shows
or art exhibits or radio and television stations. Big cities can offer a number
of events simultaneously. The major hazard is that events have to be
profitable to enjoy private support. And with city budgets tighter than ever,
less public money is available for cultural activities.

Whether the government — or private enterprise — should come to the
rescue of American cities (and whether all cities are worthy of rescue) is a
complex issue. How it is resolved, and the effect it will have on the country's
well-being, will have an effect on all Americans, wherever they live.

1492	Christopher Columbus and his crew sight land in the present-day Bahamas
1513	Ponce de León explores the coast of Florida
1565	St. Augustine, Florida, America's first European city, is founded by Pedro Menéndez
1607	Captain John Smith and 105 settlers found Jamestown, Virginia, on territory inhabited by the Powhatans, a confederacy of American Indian tribes
1609	Henry Hudson, an Englishman employed by the Dutch, sails into New York harbor
1619	The first Black laborers in the present-day U.S., termed servants, land in Jamestown
1626	Peter Minuit buys the island of Manhattan from the Manahata Indians for twenty-four dollars' worth of trinkets
1674	The Dutch cede New Amsterdam to the English, who rename it New York
1699	French settlements begin in Louisiana
1712	The first slave revolt in America takes place in New York City
1776	The Continental Congress approves the Declaration of Independence
1781	British forces surrender in Yorktown, Virginia
1803	Napoleon sells Louisiana, which stretches from the Gulf of Mexico to the Canadian border, to the U.S. for $15 million
1808	The importation of slaves is outlawed
1819	Florida is ceded to the U.S. by Spain
1835	Seminoles attack white soldiers, protesting forced removal to Oklahoma; Texas, under Sam Houston, proclaims the right to secede from Mexico
1836	Texans are wiped out by Mexican troops under General Santa Anna at the Alamo
1845	Texas admitted to the Union
1847	Mormons under Brigham Young settle Salt Lake City, Utah
1857	U.S. Supreme Court decides that a slave does not become free when taken into a free state, that Blacks could not be citizens, and that Congress could not bar slavery from a territory
1861	The Civil War begins as Confederates fire on Fort Sumter, South Carolina
1862	New Orleans falls to northern military forces
1863	Lincoln's Emancipation Proclamation frees all slaves in all states; draft riots result in one thousand deaths in New York City
1865	Lee surrenders to Grant at Appomattox Courthouse, Virginia, ending the Civil War; the Thirteenth Amendment to the U.S. Constitution outlaws slavery
1871	Fire destroys Chicago
1886	Chicago's Haymarket Riot results in deaths and injuries over labor's crusade for the eight-hour day
1892	Ellis Island opens as an immigration depot in New York
1896	The U.S. Supreme Court rules in *Plessy vs. Ferguson* that the segregation doctrine of "separate but equal" is legal, clearing the way for racially segregated public schools in the U.S.
1900	International Ladies' Garment Workers Union is founded in New York City
1903	The first transcontinental auto trip, from San Francisco to New York City, takes place

1906	The San Francisco earthquake kills more than five hundred people and causes $350 million in damage
1909	Blacks led by W.E.B. DuBois found the National Association for the Advancement of Colored People (NAACP) in New York City
1911	New York City's Triangle sweatshop fire kills 146, most of them young immigrant women
1921	Congress sharply curbs immigration
1941	The Japanese attack Pearl Harbor, and the U.S. declares war on Japan, Germany, and Italy
1942	A total of 110,000 Japanese living in the U.S., most of them Americans, are placed in detention camps by the U.S. government
1943	Race riots erupt in Detroit and in New York's Harlem
1945	World War II ends
1951	Transcontinental television begins
1954	The U.S. Supreme Court unanimously rules that segregated schools are unconstitutional
1964	A civil rights bill is passed that covers voting, jobs, and more
1965	Black rioting in the Watts section of Los Angeles leaves thirty-four dead and property losses of $200 million
1967	Vicious rioting erupts in several African-American ghettoes
1990	U.S. immigration quotas now based on number of visas granted rather than on people's national origin

GLOSSARY

agitate   to upset or disturb; frequently used to portray actions by minorities or employees who believe they are being deprived of rights or benefits

anarchy   the absence of all political authority or government

anti-Semitism   hostility toward or prejudice against Jews

beatnik   a person, particularly in the 1950s, who dresses with disregard for what is thought proper and who is a radical social critic

Bohemian   a person with literary or artistic interests who disregards conventional standards of behavior

cede   to surrender possession of

clan   a traditional unit of society, made up of a number of families claiming a common ancestor and following a chief who inherits his position

Creole   a person of various mixed ancestries: a person of European descent born in the West Indies or Spanish America; a person of French descent born in the southern U.S., especially Louisiana; a person descended from or culturally related to Spanish and Portuguese settlers of the U.S. states on the Gulf of Mexico; a person of mixed Black and European ancestry who speaks a dialect based on French or Spanish

crony   a close friend or companion

Dixieland   a style of instrumental jazz music associated with New Orleans; the music usually features horns, drums, and piano, has a strong beat, and often includes improvised solos

exotic   foreign, from another part of the world

Hasidim	a Jewish sect founded about 1750 in Poland; Hasidim live in most large North American cities
industrial revolution	social and economic changes brought on by mechanization; a major result was a shift from work at home to work in large factories
magnate	a powerful or influential person in business or industry
mogul	a member of a Muslim empire that conquered part of India in the sixteenth century; frequently, a slang word for a powerful, influential, or important person
nomad	a person with no fixed home who moves from place to place
pueblo	a community dwelling, up to five stories high, built of stone or adobe by one of several Indian tribes
republic	a constitutional form of government, usually a democratic one
Seminole	a tribe of Muskogee-speaking people of American Indian, African, and other descent; Seminoles today live in Florida
settlement house	a site in a community of newly arrived immigrants; the house and its operators teach how the society of the new country works and address other immigrant problems
smog	fog that has become mixed and polluted with automotive exhaust and other smoke
squalor	filth and misery
Underground Railroad	a secret network aiding fugitive slaves in reaching freedom in the north or Canada
union shop	a business or industry where the employees are required to be union members; also called a closed shop because employment is closed to those who refuse to join the union
utopia	any condition, place, or situation of social or political perfection
voodoo	a religion practiced in Caribbean countries, especially Haiti, that combines Roman Catholic rituals with West African religious beliefs, including the belief that a supreme God rules a host of other deities, and that believers can communicate with saints and dead ancestors through trances, dreams, and charmed objects
zydeco	popular music of southern Louisiana that combines French dance tunes, Caribbean music, and the blues; zydeco bands feature guitar, accordion, and washboard

FURTHER READING

Angelo, Frank. *Yesterday's Detroit*. Detroit: Four Press, 1993.

Brownig, Judith H. *New York City, Yesterday and Today: 30 Timeless Walking Adventures*. New York: Corsair Publications, 1992.

Cromie, Robert. *A Short History of Chicago*. San Francisco: Lexikos, 1985.

Davis, Kenneth C. *Don't Know Much About History*. New York: Avon Books, 1990.

Hardy, Phil, and Laing, David. *The Encyclopedia of Rock*. New York: MacDonald and Co., 1987.

Images of Los Angeles. Los Angeles: LTA Publications, 1991.

Peck, Abe. *Uncovering the Sixties*. New York: Pantheon Books, 1985.

Rand McNally 1993 Road Atlas. Chicago: Rand McNally, 1993.

Sachar, Howard M. *A History of the Jews in America*. New York: Knopf, 1992.

Stambler, Irwin. *The Encyclopedia of Pop, Rock and Soul*. New York: St. Martin's Press, 1989.

Zaumer, Phyllis. *San Francisco, The Way It Was, Then and Now*. San Francisco: Zanel Publications, 1980.

Zinn, Howard. *A People's History of the United States*. New York: Harper & Row, Publishers, 1980.